AF568055

THE MAN WHO SAW TOMORROW

Praise for the Book

When we think of heroes, we picture soldiers or actors. Yasaswy was different. He built a nation through education. In a rigid system where bureaucrats dictated learning, he dared to ask: Shouldn't students study what matters to the world? He fought for practical, market-ready education and won. The Institute of Chartered Financial Analysts of India (ICFAI) University stands as proof. In the 1980s, he launched India's first CFA Programme, creating financial professionals before the term was popular. To him, finance powered freedom and opportunity. A builder of institutions, Yasaswy trusted people, delegated deeply, and envisioned private enterprise long before liberalization. His message endures: dream boldly, trust others, pursue excellence. He showed India that you can fight the system—and still build something lasting.

—**Suresh Prabhu,** former Union Minister and Parliamentarian

The true measure of a man is the height of his ideals, the breadth of his sympathy, the depth of his convictions, and the length of his patience. N.J. Yasaswy held high ideals, and many looked up to him. He often challenged people to exceed their potential and pushed hard to enable them to do so. This is how he created a great institution in ICFAI. I have yet to come across someone who was not in awe of him. He was my role model during my early days and inspired me to excel in my professional exams

—P.R. Ramesh, former Chairman, Deloitte India

Yasaswy was a founder, a visionary, and a dreamer. He explained, he demonstrated, but most importantly, he inspired us to learn at IIM Ahmedabad. He invested so much energy in building this wonderful university, this foundation, and this campus. There can be no better monument to his leadership and his vision.

—Harish Bhat, former Brand Custodian, Tata Sons

I got to know N.J. Yasaswy when he founded ICFAI. Through my interactions with him as a very early member of ICFAI and later on as a member of the Board of Governors, it was fascinating to see his vision of building a world-class educational institution take shape. He provided decisive leadership to the ICFAI team which laid the foundation of a multi-disciplinary group of educational institutions across India. It was my privilege to know him.

—Anuradha Nadkarni, *Co-founder, Svakarma Finance*

N.J. Yasaswy transformed the landscape of higher education in finance and management. When India was a closed economy, he had the vision to start the CFA course in India, introducing subjects like financial engineering, derivatives, and portfolio management. As a CFA from the early batches and later as the founding Head of ICFAI Business School, Kolkata, I saw him closely for 24 years. His foresight, execution excellence, and courage to build without approval but with purpose made him unique. He was a great orator whose speeches on liberalization inspired a generation of professionals. He remains my 'Guru', who continues to inspire me to think differently and believe in my own capability—I can do.

—Kalyan Debnath, *CEO, Neotia Skill Development Academy, and former Member, Board of Governors, ICFAI*

N.J. Yasaswy is a person I will always remember for his vision, courage, and conviction in turning his ideas into enduring institutions. His flawless, no-nonsense communication and openness to new ideas attracted some of the best talent from industry and academia. I first met him in the early years of my banking career, when I was invited to the ICFAI Board in 1993. Even the most seasoned members would baulk at his 'audacious' proposals, which later proved visionary. I consider it my good fortune to have worked with him again when he started IBS Bangalore.

—Dr Lata Chakravarthy, *Adjunct Faculty, Indian Institute of Management, Bangalore*

THE MAN WHO SAW TOMORROW

THE UNTOLD STORY OF **N.J. YASASWY**, THE FOUNDER OF ICFAI

PATTABHI RAM and SUDHAKAR RAO

RUPA

Published by
Rupa Publications India Pvt. Ltd 2025
161-B/4, Gulmohar House,
Yusuf Sarai Community Centre,
New Delhi 110049

Sales centres:
Bengaluru Chennai
Hyderabad Kolkata Mumbai

P-ISBN: 978-93-7003-345-0
E-ISBN: 978-93-7003-053-4

First impression 2025

10 9 8 7 6 5 4 3 2 1

Printed in India

A man who wants to lead the orchestra must turn his back on the crowd.

—MAX LUCADO

For those who build institutions that last.

Contents

PART IV
Republic of Learning

PART V
Walking Together

PART VI
The Man

PART VII
Final Days

Foreword

I first met N.J. Yasaswy during my chartered accountancy days. Our many conversations made it clear that he would never take the conventional path. A corporate climb to a multinational CEO's chair was too small for his vision. He was destined to do something bolder. And he did.

Yasaswy chose the tougher, wiser road. He stayed in India and built something extraordinary: a multi-university platform that today spans business, technology, law and liberal arts. The ICFAI idea itself was audacious: a private, self-funded, multi-campus initiative reaching even into the less-travelled terrains of the Northeast.

On my visits to India, I saw firsthand what he had created. ICFAI is a bold *desi* experiment, modern in outlook yet deeply Indian in spirit. Yasaswy's imprint is everywhere: in its curriculum, its frugality, its discipline, and its ethos of self-reliance.

In my own work *Reverse Innovation*, I have argued that ideas must flow from emerging economies to the developed world. Yasaswy embodied that principle. His life reminds us that the future will not be invented in Silicon Valley alone. It will also be imagined in Indian classrooms.

His greatest contribution was to bring an entrepreneurial mindset into academia: taking risks, building teams, and measuring impact. He imagined when others imitated. He persisted when others paused.

I am delighted that his story is finally being told. This is the story of a man who proved that when vision meets execution, you build something that endures. For anyone who wonders whether one individual can make a difference, N.J. Yasaswy's life answers with a resounding *yes*.

—Vijay Govindarajan
Coxe Distinguished Professor
Tuck School of Business, Dartmouth College
New York Times and *Wall Street Journal* bestselling author

Abbreviations

AACSB — Association to Advance Collegiate Schools of Business
AICTE — All India Council for Technical Education
ANZ — Austaralia and New Zealand
APSFC — Andhra Pradesh State Financial Corporation
APSTC — Andhra Pradesh State Trading Corporation
ASCI — Administrative Staff College of India
BA — Bachelor of Arts
BBA — Bachelor of Business Administration
BCJ — Bar Council of India
BHEL — Bharat Heavy Electricals Limited
BITS — Birla Institute of Technology and Sciences
BPO — Busineess Process Outsourcing
BRS — Bank Reconciliation Statement
CA — Chartered Accountant
CAT — Common Admission Test
CCI — Controller of Capital Issues
CEO — Chief Executive Officer
CFA — Chartered Financial Analyst
CIFCO — Champaklal Investment and Finance Company
CIM — Chartered Institute of Management
CIMA — Chartered Institute of Management Accountants
CMA — Cost and Management Accountants
CRC — Case Research Centre
CRISIL — Credit Rating and Investment Services of India Limited

DBF	Diploma in Business Finance
DIY	Do It Yourself
DLC	Distance Learning Course
DSP	DSP Financial Consultants
EFMD	European Foundation for Management Development
ERA	Equity Research Analyst
ERP	Enterprise Resource Planning
FCA	Fellow Chartered Accountant
FDP	Faculty Development Program
GHRDC	Global Human Resource Development Centre
GMR	Grandhi Mallikarjuna Rao Group
HR	Human Resources
IAS	Indian Administrative Service
IBS	ICFAI Business School
IBSAT	ICFAI Business School Aptitude Test
ICAI	Institute of Chartered Accountants of India
ICFA	Institute of Certified Financial Analysts
ICFAI	Institute of Chartered Financial Analysts of India
ICMR	Indian Council of Medical Research
ICWA	Institute of Cost and Works Accountants
ICWAI	Institute of Cost and Works Accountants of India (now ICMAI)
IDBI	Industrial Development Bank of India
IEEE	Institute of Electrical and Electronics Engineers
IFCI	Industrial Finance Corporation of India
IFS	Indian Foreign Service
IGNOU	Indira Gandhi National Open University
IIM	Indian Institute of Management
IIMT	ICFAI Institute of Management Teachers
IIT	Indian Institute of Technology
IKC	ICFAI Knowledge Centre
INC	ICFAI National College

INSEAD	Institut Européen d'Administration des Affaires
IPCL	Indian Petrochemicals Corporation Limited
IPO	Initial Public Offering
ISIT	ICFAI School of Information Technologyy
ISMS	ICFAI School of Marketing Studies
IT	Information Technology
ITC	ITC Limited (formerly Imperial Tobacco Company of India)
ITUC	International Trade Union Confederation
JEE	Joint Entrance Examination
JLR	Jaguar Land Rover
JNTU	Jawaharlal Nehru Technological University
KBR	Kellogg Brown & Root
LIC	Life Insurance Corporation
LLB	Legum Baccalaureus (Bachelor of Law)
LSE	London School of Economics
LTTE	Liberation Tigers of Tamil Eelam
MBA	Master of Business Administration
MBFS	Mercahant Banking and Financial Services
MDP	Management Development Programme
MENA	Middle East and North Africa
MFC	Master of Finance and Control
MIS	Management Information Systems
MLA	Member of the Legislative Assembly
MSB	Magnus School of Business
NABARD	National Bank for Agriculture and Rural Development
NASA	National Aeronautics and Space Administration
NDA	Non-Disclosure Agreement
NEP	National Education Policy
NMIMS	Narsee Monjee Institute of Management Studies
NTR	Nandamuri Taraka Rama Rao
ONGC	Oil and Natural Gas Compnay

OU	Open University
PC	Personal Computer
PFM	Personal Financial Management
PGDBM	Post Graduate Diploma in Business Management
PGDM	Post Graduate Diploma in Management
PIL	Public Interest Litigation
PIN	Postal Indication Number
PSU	Public Sector Undertaking
QCBS	Quality and Cost-Based Selection
RAW	Research and Analysis Wing
RBI	Reserve Bank of India
RO	Regional Office
RSTA	Registrar and Share Transfer Agency
SBI	State Bank of India
SEBI	Securities and Exchange Board of India
SICASA	Southern India Chartered Accountants Students Association
SLA	Service Level Agreement
SLV	Satellite Launch Vehicle
SRC	Securities Research Centre
TAPMI	TA Pai Management Institute
TCS	Tata Consultancy Services
TFM	Treasury and Forex Management
TOI	Times Of India
TV	Television
UCLA	University of California, Los Angeles
UGC	University Grants Commision
UK	United Kingdom
USA	United States of America
UTI	Unit Trust of India
XLRI	Xavier Labour Relations Institute
YMA	Yasaswy Management Associates

Preface

The 'University' lives on long after he is gone.

To those who worked with him, N.J. Yasaswy was more a mentor—he was their North Star—always constant, always pointing the way.

He never received a Padma award. He didn't appear on magazine covers or television panels. Outside academic circles, many may not even know him. Today's generation has no idea of the man he was.

But Yasaswy preferred it that way. He stayed away from the spotlights, saying: 'The work must speak louder than the man.'

And oh, what work it was.

Yasaswy was far ahead of his time. His ideas became institutions. Those institutions became templates. Today, thousands of students walk through campuses he once imagined in silence—and built, brick by red brick.

So how does a schoolteacher's son from a dusty district headquarters—Guntur in Andhra Pradesh—build a national university network? How does he do it without political connections, government recognition, or public funding? And how does he achieve it all in just 25 years?

This story deserves to be told—with honesty and in its entirety—so that future generations may come to know of him. That's why we're writing this book. In these pages, you'll read about his victories and failures, his big bets and his strategic retreats. If we focused only on the highs and skipped the lows, we wouldn't just fail you—we'd fail him.

Yasaswy wasn't a typical entrepreneur. He didn't pitch to investors or pose for photographs at summits. He didn't play stud poker—no bluff, no bravado. But he went all out: on new programmes, new markets, and new institutions. Many didn't work. But the ones that did, soared.

He was a fighter. When regulations blocked his way, he built a new gate by founding India's first chain of private universities.

He wasn't perfect, but he was rare—the kind who showed others how institutions should be built. His cardinal principles were systems before slogans, depth before dazzle, and purpose before personal brand.

We interviewed over 75 people—family, friends, colleagues and critics. What emerged wasn't the tale of a superhero. It was something rarer: the story of a man who never tired, who kept showing up. A man who proved deep focus can build great institutions.

In an age addicted to noise, Yasaswy practised silence—a silence worth listening to.

If there ever was a time to remember him, it would be now—2025. This is the fortieth year of his creation, the Institute of Chartered Financial Analysts of India (ICFAI); the thirtieth year of his masterpiece, the IFCAI Business School (IBS); and the twenty-fifth year of his proudest legacy, the Case Research Centre (CRC). Above all, it is the seventy-fifth year of his birth.

This isn't a feel-good tribute. It's a guide for those who want to imagine, work, and build institutions that last a thousand years.

Let's begin.

Prologue

The Charminar in Hyderabad is one of India's best-known monuments. The nearly four-hundred-year-old mosque above and the crowded bazaars below make it a must-see.

In 1994, a few kilometres away from this landmark, a group of men gathered in a quiet hotel. They were part of an educational institution that had punched beyond its weight during the previous decade.

Among them was a bespectacled strategist who thought in frameworks. Next to him was a forty-year-old in a crisp suit, looking hungry for success. Across from them sat a middle-aged banker with his legs crossed. Four more people made up the group of seven.

There was anxiety in the air.

'We've built something good so far. Why should we mess with it?' one of them asked.

'But think of the opportunities it can throw up.'

The banker offered no comment. He was poker-faced, like most bankers.

Then the man in the light blue shirt spoke. 'Good isn't enough. We need to break new ground. We must move to greatness.'

He had a magnetic appeal and the habit of saying something quietly that made people rethink their position.

'Diversification is not a distraction. It's a defence.' he explained. 'We can't be a one-product organization. The world won't wait for us. We must ringfence ourselves with more products.'

The strategist raised his hand. 'What about core competence?' He and a friend had recently attended a seminar where management gurus Gary Hamel and C.K. Prahalad had spoken on this theory. Hamel and Prahalad's core competence theory calls for firms to focus on what they do particularly well. In contrast, diversification spreads a firm across several businesses and dilutes focus unless built around those strengths.

The discussion continued, with each man contributing his thoughts. It lasted seventy-five minutes. Gradually, they warmed up to the idea of starting the business school.

It was late in the day. They had reached an agreement, and so it was time to leave.

That's when the man in the blue shirt announced a plan that truly stretched the elastic band of reality.

'We'll start nine business schools,' he said, his eyes dancing. 'In eight cities. And we will do it all in one shot.'

The group gasped in disbelief. They had initially resisted one dish, and now the man served them a plateful!

'We're not ready for even one,' a member protested.

'We don't have the people,' said another.

'It's too much.'

He, in the blue shirt, waved off their concerns. 'We'll figure it out. We always do, don't we?'

The chairman, Dr A. Besant C. Raj, silent till then, looked around the room. 'N.J. Yasaswy is operationally in charge and runs the show. Let's trust his instinct.'

That was the final word.

In 1994, Hyderabad was far from the global IT powerhouse it is today. The airport was at Begumpet; HITEC City was not yet born; Gachibowli was a nondescript suburb, and there was no Outer Ring Road. Cyberabad, with its PIN code 500081, had yet to emerge.

At that moment, unbeknown to them, this group of men had set in motion a chain of events that would rewrite the game. History, as always, took its time catching up.

Days later, the Board gave its nod. A list was drawn: Ahmedabad, Bangalore, Bombay, Calcutta, Madras, New Delhi, Pune, and Hyderabad.

Eight cities, nine campuses. The capital city would have an additional campus at Mehrauli.

A quizmaster would pin these places on a map three decades later and ask, 'What connects them?'

PART I

Finding His Feet

Great men are meteors designed to burn
so that the earth may be lighted.

—NAPOLEON BONAPARTE

PART I

Finding His Feet

Great men are meteors designed to burn
so that the earth may be lighted.

—NAPOLEON BONAPARTE

Chapter 1

The Boy from Guntur

It was 26 January 1950, the first day of a new era. Fireworks lit up New Delhi as India cut itself loose from the British monarchy and stepped out as a sovereign republic—head held high and heart full of hope.

A fortnight later, on 9 February, a different dream began in Guntur, Andhra Pradesh. A boy was born to Nandury Venkateswara Rao, a schoolteacher, and his wife Seetharamamma (Seetha) Nandury, a homemaker.

They named him Yasaswy, the Sanskrit word for 'famous'.

One Sunday afternoon, Yasaswy, barely eleven months old, held on to the coffee table and took a few wobbly steps forward. *Nanna Garu*—Venkateswara Rao—was in his favourite chair, holding a coffee tumbler.

Just then, the doorbell rang.

Without looking up, Seetha, who was working in the kitchen, said, 'Babu, see who is at the door.'

With a sparkle in his eye, little Babu let go of the table and toddled across the floor. Standing outside was a woman in a white sari, her head wrapped in a pallu, like the widows in the 1950s.

Without a word, for he hadn't learnt to speak, Babu lumbered across to a pile of clothes, pulled out a piece of white fabric, and draped it over his head.

Nanna Garu burst out laughing. 'Seetha! Look at him! So very observant!'

Seetha beamed. 'I think he'll grow up to be exceptionally sharp.'

'*Avunu* (yes).'

That tiny act of mimicry was the first glimpse of a mind that observed deeply and acted instantly.

Nandury J. Yasaswy—Babu—was the apple of his parents' eyes. In the years to come, he would conceptualize, nurture and grow a multi-university empire. But that was still years away. For now, he was a bright little kid in a small town.

⁂

When Yasaswy turned six, Nanna Garu introduced him to *Chandamama* and *Balamitra*, magazines that were popular among children then. Slowly, the boy's collections increased, and he soon built a library.

'Here's the latest *Chandamama*,' Nanna said each time he handed over a copy.

'Thank you! Thank you!' Yasaswy would squeal, flipping the pages. 'I'll share it with my friends!' That urge to share knowledge had come early.

Soon, he started lending books and began tracking them in a ruled notebook.

'Can I borrow this?' a friend would ask.

'Sure. But return it on time,' he'd say, noting it down like a tiny librarian.

Every book was documented. He wrote down when his father gave him the book, whether he had finished reading, to whom he had lent, on what date, and whether the borrower had returned it. The audit instinct had already kicked in!

As someone said later, 'He was born with the precision of an auditor and the big-picture thinking of an institution builder.'

⁂

The boy wasn't one to take things lying down. It showed up early during a rubber ball incident.

Yasaswy had a collection of rubber balls that older kids in the neighbourhood liked. They would come to his house, take one, and play with it. Some days, they would let him join in, and on other days, they wouldn't.

Once, a boy asked, 'Why aren't you joining us?'

'I don't know,' he said, holding back his hurt.

As the game continued, Yasaswy calmly collected the balls from those playing with it, walked into the house, and bolted the door.

His mother noticed him and asked, 'Are you okay?'

'I'm tired of watching from the sidelines,' he said, his eyes soft.

'You shouldn't feel left out, Babu. Their actions don't define your worth.'

He never forgot that line. 'Their actions don't define your worth.'

Even as a boy, Yasaswy had figured out one of life's unwritten rules: When the world sidelines you, don't sulk. Step aside with dignity.

❧

Guntur lies on the banks of the Krishna River. It boasts of a long lineage of Indian rulers, from the Satavahanas to the Kakatiyas, followed by the Mughals and later the British.

As a boy, Yasaswy loved walking on the roads. The place bustled with chilli, cotton, and tobacco markets. These markets taught him the essence of hard work. Guntur thrived on spicy food, and Yasaswy was known to eat raw red chillies!

The town's schools and universities piqued Yasaswy's curiosity. The Amaravati Stupa, built in the Buddhist era and a Guntur landmark, served as his moral compass.

No one knew that one day this boy would build institutions across India. But the signs were already visible—in his notebooks, in his quiet resolve to be respected, and in the way he once foxed a traffic constable.

Yes, the ingredients were already in place. They just needed time to simmer.

First among Friends

Sri Majety Guravaiah High School (MGHS) has stood in Guntur since 1945. That's where young Yasaswy studied, surrounded by four boys who would become lifelong friends. They were Hanumantha Rao, Brihaspati Vavilala, M. Sivakumar, and K.V. Ravula.

The boys laughed, argued, and played together. Years later, life would scatter them around: Rao went off to IIT, Vavilala to XLRI, Sivakumar opted for agriculture, while Ravula got into insurance. Yasaswy chose finance.

'We were a bunch of wide-eyed kids at school, eager to explore the world,' Rao recalls. 'But Yasaswy? Even back then, you could sense he was someone special.'

Sivakumar remembers the first time he heard the name: 'When I joined Class 6A, everyone talked about a boy named Yasaswy. He was the son of our math teacher, Venkateswara Rao Garu, and studied in Class 6B. While we topped our sections, he topped the entire class—every year, year after year, without fail.'

No wonder he was hugely popular and elected Monitor. The charisma for which he would later become known was already evident.

At twelve, Yasaswy translated an English biography of Abraham Lincoln into Telugu. Years later, a giant portrait of Lincoln would hang on his office wall like a guiding compass.

'Those were magical years,' Rao said. 'And Yasaswy...he was the brightest star in our constellation.'

When their English teacher, Ramalingayya Garu, launched a class magazine called *Vani*, Yasaswy, then fifteen, was made editor. He handled deadlines, edits, layout, and proofing with rare calm. Rao was his deputy.

Then came the traffic incident where he foxed a cop.

⁂

The sun was descending into the Krishna. Yasaswy was cycling down the road, with a friend riding pillion, cracking jokes. There was no dynamo on the bike, no care in the world, until a policeman flagged them down for the missing dynamo. 'Name?' the policeman barked.

Yasaswy didn't bat an eyelid. 'I'm Banerjee. He's Mukherjee.' He didn't want his parents to find out about his tryst with the law.

Two Telugu boys suddenly turned Bengali. How would anyone believe it? Well, the cop did, and that's all that mattered.

The next day, 'Banerjee and Mukherjee' showed up at court. The moment Yasaswy saw the magistrate, he froze.

It turned out the magistrate lived in their building. He was friends with Yasaswy's father. And yes, the man loved sharing courtroom stories over coffee. That's how the news reached home. The duo was fined two rupees each.

Seetha was furious. Even then, when she retold the story within the family, there was a sly smile and the mother's pride at her son's clever ruse.

Clearly Yasaswy had been willing to take risks. Somewhere in there was a lesson. That you must think on your feet. That you must network. After all, had he not been his father's son, the magistrate might have taken a dimmer view.

⁂

By now, Yasaswy's curiosity had turned into hunger—the kind that no classroom could fully contain.

Later, in SSLC, the school-leaving exam, he stood second in the state. It was the only time he didn't finish first. But more of that later.

While the toppers rushed to become doctors or engineers, Yasaswy chose commerce because it led to a career in chartered accountancy. 'I want to find solutions for the poor, and finance will help me do that,' he told his friends. For him, numbers were tools to move the world.

He wasn't ducking science, though. Rao remembered a moment. 'I was at IIT. One day, seventeen-year-old Yasaswy showed me a solution to a geometry theorem using the segment of a triangle. It was simply elegant. You don't expect that level of clarity at that age.'

Yasaswy joined Hindu College in Guntur to earn his BCom. Economics, accounting, and taxation were subjects he loved and mastered. He also set his sights on completing both ICWA and CA.

But first, he had to get the address of the Institute of Cost and Works Accountants of India (ICWAI). That took him months. In the pre-Google world, persistence was your best search engine.

College unlocked another of his gifts, public speaking. He hit the debate circuit. His voice was mesmeric, his thinking razor-sharp, and his memory annoyingly good.

Brihaspati led the Telugu debates, while Yasaswy took charge in English. They were like the Wes Hall and Charlie Griffith of the circuit, backed by R. Vittal and M. Dattatreya. They argued on stage, won their share of cups, and laughed hard over late-night meals in hotels.

Books were his other world. He read everything: from economics, politics, philosophy, law, to religion. Before graduating, he had already read Adam Smith's *The Wealth of Nations*.

Years later, those ideas would reappear—repackaged and refreshed—and delivered in auditoriums across India.

He helped people quietly. 'When we joined Hindu College,' Sivakumar recalled, 'he told me to pick Hindi as a second language because it came with a scholarship. That one tip saved my family real money.'

When the graduation results came in, Yasaswy had topped the university. His friends weren't surprised. And for him, it was like another box ticked.

Scholar on Fourth Lane

Each night, after supper, the friends would gather under the flickering streetlight on Fourth Lane in Brodipet. In the PST (post-supper talks), they discussed everything under the sun, and sometimes the sun itself. Yasaswy introduced topics he considered as being of national interest!

'Why do you think this matters for India's future?' he'd ask, half-grin in place. What began as a monologue often turned into a spirited debate. His friends became sparring partners in politics, philosophy, economics, and other subjects.

During the Sino-Indian war of 1962, one of them asked, 'Why are they fighting in the snow?'

'Because that's where the border is,' Yasaswy said, deadpan. 'High up in the Himalayas.'

'But weren't we friends with China?'

'We were. Then both sides claimed the same land.'

'Couldn't they just share it?'

'Mountains don't work like that,' Yasaswy shrugged. 'You either hold them, or you don't.'

And so, night after night, the Brodipet quartet debated

the world as if it were theirs to fix. Some comments were insightful, some nonsensical, but no one wanted to miss it. That street corner became Brodipet's own think tank, with Yasaswy as its restless moderator.

He wasn't just a scholar under the streetlights. He had quirks, too.

M.S. Raghavan Ayyangar, his neighbour, remembered their 4 a.m. standoffs at the municipal tap.

'Yasaswy would never let me go first,' he laughed. 'We argued every morning. He insisted on filling his vessels before I got a drop.'

Their families were close. Yasaswy's mother, Seetha, and Raghavan's sister, Kamala, had studied together. 'He loved Kamala's cooking,' Raghavan recalled. 'He called it *Mangamma Gaari Vantalu*—Mangamma's meals—a phrase that would become shorthand for comfort and warmth.

After graduation, Yasaswy went on to pursue both Chartered and Cost Accountancy.

He became something of a legend at the Southern India Chartered Accountants Students Association (SICASA) events. At the All-India CA Students Conference in Chennai, he dismantled the Companies Act and Income Tax Act with the ease of a professor.

In Brahmayya & Co., where he did CA articleship, colleagues watched him interpret financial ratios like a forensic analyst. He radiated mastery, and so, no one was surprised when he topped India in the CA Intermediate exam. Yes, he finished All-India first.

His friend Sivakumar remembers hosting Yasaswy in New Delhi when the latter flew in to receive his gold medal. Friends lined up to meet the topper, but Yasaswy remained calm, almost unaffected. That was his rhythm—achieve, absorb, move on.

But he never forgot to lift others. Brihaspati and Umapati were brothers. One afternoon, at Brihaspati's home, Yasaswy turned to their father. 'Please let Umapati try CA.'

When the time came to take the exams, he asked Umapati to shift to Chennai and offered him his hostel room. For the younger boy, being seen with the star student felt like walking on air.

In 1972, the legal luminary Nani Palkhivala came to Chennai to speak on the Union Budget. A week before the event, Yasaswy read every article he could find. Mark it; he hadn't even cleared CA Intermediate yet.

He and Umapati arrived at the auditorium early, grabbed front-row seats, and stayed back to meet the legend. Yasaswy asked a few questions, listened carefully, and then added his own thoughts.

Palkhivala, pretty impressed, patted him on the back. 'You must start giving budget speeches, once you're done with CA.'

Winning such recognition at twenty-two was a significant high. In later years, Yasaswy would take the stage to unpack the union budget analyses before packed auditorium, making economics sound like poetry. The audience loved his wit and wisdom.

Yasaswy grew up in a household that took values seriously. From his father, he learned discipline, and from his mother, patience. Both taught him a quiet calm that made people stop and listen.

But even his closest friends admit he kept his inner world to himself, as was obvious in July 1973 at *The Indian Express* office in Vijayawada where they had gone for the CA Final results. Brihaspati recalls it.

The teleprinter crackled. Names rolled out. Then came the rank list. At the top was Nandury J. Yasaswy. Brihaspati leapt in joy. Yasaswy stood Buddha-like. There was no cheer, no fist pump, just a gentle nod. As if he had simply ticked off an item on his bucket list.

There's another story people love to tell.

Months earlier, N.J. Yasaswy and Vijay Govindarajan, both frontrunners, tossed a coin to decide who would take the CA final exam first. Because both wanted to win the gold medal.

Govindarajan won the toss and wrote the exam in November '72. He finished first. Yasaswy followed in May '73. He, too, finished first.

Govindarajan would go on to become a global strategy professor, and Yasaswy would build the ICFAI Group.

Years later, when asked about the tossing of the coin, Yasaswy smiled, neither confirming nor denying anything. And so, the fable lives on.

Yasaswy also topped the intermediate and final exams of the ICWAI, making it five national top ranks. Fifty years on, no one has matched that record. It is India's academic equivalent of Bradman's 99.94 batting average—impossible to beat.

India's top head-hunter, Francis Menzies, wanted the boy wonder for Tata Consultancy Services (TCS). But in a move that surprised many, Yasaswy joined ITC in Guntur and later the Administrative Staff College of India (ASCI) in Hyderabad.

This time, the script he was writing was his own.

CHAPTER 2

The First Handshake

1973

The Yom Kippur War had broken out, America stood behind Israel, and a retaliatory Arab oil embargo sent shockwaves through the world. Wimbledon reeled under a dramatic boycott over Nikola Pilić and a 6-feet 4-inches, wiry Indian named Vijay Amritraj was making waves on global tennis courts.

Far away from these tremors, in Hyderabad, something else was stirring.

At the ASCI, Dr Besant C. Raj, the college's top consultant, flipped through a research paper. ASCI had recently established its research arm and was looking to engage sharp minds.

A colleague walked in, tea cup in hand, the steam still playing curls.

'Have you heard of this young lad from Guntur?' he asked. 'N.J. Yasaswy. Five gold medals. He's with ITC now.'

Raj looked up, scratched his nose, and said, 'Interesting. Let's reach out to him.'

'I doubt he'll say yes. Why would someone leave ITC to join a teaching institute?'

Raj smiled faintly. 'Maybe he will. Maybe he won't. We have nothing to lose. Isn't it?'

A letter went out to Yasaswy from Raj's desk, suggesting a

meeting on any convenient date. No one expected a response.

Within a week, a young man in a blue shirt walked into Raj's office.

The handshake was firm, the smile reserved, and it turned to be the beginning of a lifelong partnership.

'Welcome,' Raj said, gesturing to the chair.

The two spoke for over an hour, not just about the job but also about goals, values, and what it meant to teach.

Finally, Raj came to the point. 'Corporate life has huge rewards. Prestige and money are two of them. You are immensely talented, and I am sure you will go places. But if you want to make a lasting impact, you must teach. It is the classroom that changes people.'

Yasaswy was quiet for a moment. The point wasn't new. His father, after all, was a schoolteacher and commanded immense respect.

He thought for a few seconds. He had the charm, gravitas, and skill to become the czar at ITC one day.

Then he said slowly, each word measured. 'My college teacher once told me to follow the path that feeds your soul, not just your wallet.'

Raj waited for Yasaswy's next sentence.

The lad, eighteen years younger, met Raj's eyes. 'I'm in.'

The ebony-coloured professor with thick spectacles extended his hand. 'Then let's get to work.'

And so it began.

In 1974, as India tested its first nuclear device at Pokhran, Yasaswy stepped into a classroom, armed with ideas. He began teaching finance to India's corporate managers. From then on, he grew close to Raj though a generation separated them.

Raj knew what it meant to walk off the beaten path. He

had started his academic life teaching psychology and logic. Somewhere along the way, curiosity pulled him into finance.

The journey took him first to the classrooms of IIM Ahmedabad as a student and later to Harvard, where he was a doctoral scholar. By 1970, PhD in hand, he was back in India as head of the finance area at ASCI—his lectures now more about cash flow than Carl Jung.

In those early days, Yasaswy often sat quietly in the back rows, listening, taking notes, and figuring out what worked and what didn't. Raj's clarity of thought and his gift of using of simple, relatable examples to explain complex theory drew Yasaswy in. In Raj, he saw the very virtues he would later practise himself: precision and the quiet courage to move beyond one's first discipline.

Once, in a quiet moment, he admitted to Raj, 'I don't know half the things you talk about.' Yes, the country's top-ranking accountant told the former psychology professor that he was unaware of the many concepts the latter taught.

Raj broke the truth with care. 'You know more accounting than anyone I've met. But corporate finance? Yes, that's a different cup of coffee.'

It was the first of their many conversations about calm in the face of chaos.

Change was already in the air, and Yasaswy could sense it. The listener had turned thinker now; he was beginning to question the syllabus. 'Our training is outdated,' he told Raj. 'What we teach must match what the market will soon demand.'

The two began to dream out loud. They spoke of setting up an institute where finance would be taught as a craft, not just a curriculum; an institute similar to the ICAI but teaching capital markets.

'God willing,' they agreed, 'we'll build it one day.'

In class, Yasaswy was a revelation. He taught the course 'Finance for Non-Finance Executives' in a sharp, witty style. He simplified jargon without dumbing it down.

Once, during a session on capital budgeting, a participant asked, 'Why should we discount future cash flows if there's no inflation?' At the time, some countries had zero inflation.

Yasaswy paused, cleared his throat, and said, 'The discount rate isn't just about inflation; it's the opportunity cost. It's what you give up by saying yes to this project when you could have said yes to another.'

The course was a hit at ASCI, and Yasaswy was its rock star.

Consulting offers followed. Industrialists who attended the course returned with projects. Dr K.V.K. Raju of Nagarjuna Group became a client, and eventually a friend. So did Nrupendra Rao of Pennar Steels, whom Yasaswy later helped steer through a restructuring.

Soon, a third person joined Raj and Yasaswy.

His name was Prasanna Chandra. A gold medallist in finance, he was possibly the only man in history to quit a bank job after just one day in office. At the time, he was teaching at Osmania University. His roots ran deep in capital markets—his grandfather had helped set up the Hyderabad Stock Exchange in the 1940s and had traded in stocks well into his nineties.

Yasaswy sketched a blueprint for an Indian Wharton focused on finance. But the timing wasn't right yet.

Meanwhile, Chandra left for XLRI, then the US, and finally started teaching at IIM Bangalore. Raj moved to Madras and became a full-time consultant. In 1980, after six intense years at ASCI, Yasaswy completed the trilogy of exits. He set up Yasaswy Management Associates (YMA) in Hyderabad, tugged by the pull of entrepreneurship.

For four years, things were silent. Then, in 1984, the seed

finally sprouted, and ICFAI was born. It would totally change how India saw financial education. But the real story, as we know, began a decade earlier, when an ambitious lad in a blue shirt walked into a modest office, and a professor with a gentle smile offered him a chair.

Hijacked, August 1982

Siva Ram Mallela was one of Yasaswy's earliest mentees. In May 1982, Yasaswy hired chartered accountants who could work on computer-based systems. Siva Ram applied, sat across from him for an interview, and was selected.

Yasaswy had flown to Northwestern University a few months earlier to pursue a PhD. He came back in twenty-four days. 'They want me to build theories,' he said, half-laughing. 'I want to build things.'

There were just three of them at YMA, but 'it felt like a lab of revolutionaries. Yasaswy handed out management ideas like secret blueprints.'

'We felt like Columbus, with calculators,' Siva Ram would later say.

Then came his trial by fire.

Siva Ram was to deliver a training session at Hindustan Zinc, Udaipur. The room was full of seasoned executives. He walked in, and his nerves walked out. He froze, fumbled, and failed.

Yasaswy just smiled. The kind of smile that said, 'You tripped. So what? Stand up.'

The two flew back the next day, Udaipur to Hyderabad via Delhi. It was 20 August 1982, a day no one on that Indian Airlines flight would forget.

They were seated in the last row. 'I counted seventy passengers,' Siva Ram would recall. You see, an accountant is trained to count. Yasaswy, as usual, was holding court with jokes, insights, and the odd wisecrack.

Then came the sound—a click. A sardar emerged from the restroom, eyes sharp. He called over the airhostess, and pulled a pistol on her.

'Cockpit,' he said.

Minutes later, the captain's voice filled the cabin.

'Ladies and gentlemen, our flight has been hijacked. We've been instructed to proceed to Libya. Please stay calm.'

Calm? Try telling that to the pregnant passenger who fainted in her seat. Or the hijacker, who marched everyone to the back row like a cattle drive.

The aircraft circled forty-two times before touching down, not in Libya but Amritsar. The Indian government had foxed the hijacker.

That should've been the end. But the nightmare had just begun. The plane was almost out of fuel, so the air conditioning was shut down. The toilets overflowed, a child screamed, and someone vomited. The air was thick with helplessness.

'If my demands aren't met, this plane goes down,' the hijacker said.

He wanted Khalistan supporters released and a public apology from Mrs Indira Gandhi. Desperation began to creep in. How long can you sit inside an aircraft?

Finally, passengers were allowed to approach the open door to breathe. Siva Ram was first in line. The hijacker stood beside him, pistol in hand.

Someone shoved the hijacker from behind. He stumbled, his hands shook, and the pistol went off. Luckily, no one was hurt.

Suddenly, the emergency exit was flung open. 'Jump!' they shouted.'

Yasaswy looked at Siva Ram. 'Go,' he screamed.

'Come with me, Sir.'

He shook his head. An old man had collapsed nearby. Yasaswy stepped toward him, shielding him with his body and waving others past. He wouldn't leave that man behind.

Real leaders don't always charge ahead. Sometimes they stand back, because someone else can't. That day, Yasaswy didn't talk about courage. He chose to be courageous.

It was what made him fearless—whether while launching private placements in a grey zone or while setting up universities in a maze of regulations. When the rules blurred, he saw through the fog in. He could argue with regulators like a philosopher wearing courtroom robes—calm, articulate and persuasive. He didn't shout orders or bend the rules; he just pointed to the path ahead, and walked it first. With Yasaswy around, even a hijack couldn't shake you: somehow he made meaning out of madness.

That courage would soon find a larger stage. The man who had stayed calm in a hijack would build institutions in a storm.

Chapter 3

Magic and Meltdown

In the 1980s, matinee idol N.T. Rama Rao (a.k.a. NTR) was Andhra Pradesh's Chief Minister. Popular and flamboyant, he was a dream merchant. He wanted his MLAs to understand finance.

'If there's anyone who can talk money, it's N.J. Yasaswy,' someone told him. That's how 'capital' met 'charisma'. What emerged was a full-blown display of why Yasaswy came to be known as the wizard of finance.

Yasaswy delivered a series of electrifying sessions for the MLAs that had NTR floored.

'Join me full-time,' he said. 'I'll make you cabinet minister.'

Yasaswy declined gently. 'Sir, my clients and consulting work need me. In any case, I'm always available for you.'

NTR wouldn't give up easily. Sometime later, he offered him the chairmanship of the Andhra Pradesh State Trading Corporation (APSTC), a floundering public enterprise on life support. This time, Yasaswy could not say no because it was about Andhra's pride.

He walked in with a briefcase of ideas. With his managing director, Anwar, he injected hire-purchase and leasing into the veins of APSTC. The bottom line turned from red to black, and people started noticing.

One day, on Yasaswy's advice, Siva Ram decided to use the downtime to research on taxation of bonus issues. It led him to write a comprehensive article on the topic. Impressed, Yasaswy asked him to write for the firm.

Thus, Siva Ram began contributing to *Invest India*, YMA's monthly magazine, and *Hifco Investment Advice*, the weekly newsletter. Every Friday night, the lights at YMA burned past midnight. While Hyderabad slept, they crunched Bombay Stock Exchange data, extracted insights, and sent out crisp commentary by Saturday morning

V.R. Sankara joined him on these late-night grind sessions. Quiet, methodical, and razor-sharp, he would one day rise to the uppermost echelons of the institution Yasaswy was building.

Yasaswy didn't train them. He simply raised the bar and watched them reach for it.

An Idea Is Born

The boardroom smelled of South Indian filter coffee. K.V.K. Raju sat at the head of the table, restless. The government had decontrolled steel; this was the time to expand Nagarjuna Steel. IDBI, was ready to fund, but wanted Raju to bring in matching capital as promoters' equity

He turned to Yasaswy. 'What do we do?'

Yasaswy tapped his pen on the desk. Then, with zero drama, he said, 'We ask our readers.'

He was referring to his newsletter subscribers—four thousand of them. He grabbed a sheet and scribbled out a simple letter. *Would you like to invest in Nagarjuna Steel* he asked them in that mail.

Soon, envelopes came flooding in, and just like that the promoter's quota was fully subscribed.

Raju was over the moon.

Then a question arose: 'Who's a promoter? Can there be so many promoters?'

Siva Ram dug into Section 67(c) of the Companies Act. It wasn't helpful.

Yasaswy looked at the silence in the law and interpreted it generously. 'Promoter didn't just mean one or two people. It meant family, friends, and well-wishers—anyone who believes.'

And just like that, the Indian concept of private placement was born. Not in Parliament, but in a boardroom where a consultant happened to sit. Nagarjuna Steels had pioneered it. Soon, it became the go-to strategy for others to follow.

In Bangalore, Yasaswy encouraged two IIM graduates, Sampath and Santhanam, to enter entrepreneurship. 'Float a leasing company,' he said.

They did. Thus, Bangalore Leasing Ltd was born, along with a twin company that would cross-invest to fill the promoter's quota.

The strategy was sharp, maybe with a shade of grey, but Yasaswy believed what was not expressly prohibited was implicitly allowed. His famous quip was, 'There's the legal approach to law. And there's the case law approach to law.'

By 1983, the model was everywhere: Nagarjuna Finance, Nagarjuna Investment Trust, First Growth Fund, and Midwest Leasing followed—each with trusted faces at the helm and private placements at their core.

Each success raised Yasaswy's credentials, and he became the man whose ideas raised capital and built trust and loyalty.

The Five-Finger Plan

At the breakfast table at Taj Intercontinental in Mumbai, conversations hummed.

In a quiet corner sat Yasaswy, C.D. Ramachandran, stockbroker Bhagirath Merchant and Siva Ram.

'Kaisa Hai?' (How's everything?) Yasaswy asked Merchant in hesitant Hindi.

'Badiya Hai,' (All good) Merchant smiled. He was a celebrated merchant banker.

Then Yasaswy raised his hand and spread his five fingers. *Paanch*. Merchant blinked. Before he could speak, Ramachandran said, 'Yes, it's possible.'

Midwest Leasing wanted to raise its capital from ₹1 crore to ₹5 crore.

Not one to waste time, Yasaswy asked Siva Ram, 'How long will it take?'

'A week,' he replied, secretly hoping for two weeks.

'Tomorrow,' said the boss.

Siva Ram panicked. 'Sir... the paperwork has to be readied.'

'That's your problem! Catch the next flight to New Delhi. Meet the Controller of Capital Issues (CCI).'

Siva Ram left his half-eaten idli, grabbed a clean shirt, and raced to the airport. There was no time for logic, only raw faith.

At the counter, he hit a wall. Those were the days of open tickets, where you bought a ticket from the airline without a date and then got yourself a confirmation at the airport.

The agent looked up and said, 'No seats, Sir.'

An officer had to pencil in an 'OK' on the open ticket to confirm the booking. Siva Ram, sweating, stepped aside and pulled out a pen. He hesitated, then scribbled. What else could he do?

The agent issued the boarding pass, and Siva Ram boarded the next flight. You had got to do whatever it takes.

In Delhi, he walked into the office of B.S. Maniyam, Deputy Secretary at the Controller of Capital Issues.

'I need this cleared by tomorrow,' he said, placing the case before the officer.

'Where's the application?'

'Give me a paper. I'll write it now!'

The file moved through bureaucracy's snakes and ladders until it reached the top man by the next morning. Siva Ram sat outside the CCI head's office and grabbed the papers the moment they were signed. He then rushed to the airport and was back in Hyderabad by evening.

He walked straight into Yasaswy's office.

'Got it.'

Yasaswy smiled. That barely-there ghost of a smile. 'Good work.'

Five crores wouldn't raise an eyebrow today. But back then, it could turn a whole company around. For Yasaswy it wasn't about the money; it was about momentum. The next assignment was already waiting.

The Ritz Lesson

'Fly to Mumbai,' Yasaswy told Siva Ram. 'Handle the Larsvin Finance issue. Talk to CIFCO and DSP. Stay at the Taj.'

Siva Ram travelled to the country's financial capital with Anand Rao, the promoter. They checked into the Ritz.

CIFCO was the steamroller of the public issue market at the time, and DSP Financial Consultants had access to top investors who could ensure the issue was fully subscribed.

Neither of them was willing to meet the duo. They tried TCS, but the Tata company didn't bother. Only Oberoi, the Nirma genius, agreed, and that too barely so.

Back in Hyderabad, they gave Yasaswy the update. When Yasaswy heard 'Ritz,' he froze.

'The Ritz?' he asked.

'Yes, Sir. It looked clean and inexpensive.'

'We're not tourists, Siva Ram.' Yasaswy said, voice calm. In fact, too calm.

Then came the line that became a legend: 'You have to do business the way business has to be done. Not the way you want to do it.'

He wasn't talking about hotels; he was talking about mindset.

To Yasaswy, even the selection of a hotel was about brand positioning. Where you stayed mattered because it signalled who you were. The Ritz was economical, but the Taj signalled presence.

'Go back to Mumbai. Stay at the Taj. Start again.'

This time Siva Ram and Rao checked into the Taj. The shift was immediate.

Calls were returned, meetings scheduled, DSP and CIFCO opened their doors, and TCS sent consultants to discuss RSTA services. Siva Ram even met F.C. Kohli, the father of Indian Information Technology industry.

The Big Man extended a hand. 'We want to work with companies like yours.'

Back in Hyderabad, Siva Ram said, 'It's done. Larsvin is going public.'

Yasaswy nodded. 'Good.'

Siva Ram remembered: 'You have to do business the way business has to be done.'

But what happens when you don't know the rules of the game? When you walk into a world you don't fully understand? Read on...

Manufacturing Meltdowns

The magic years didn't last. Success breeds hunger, and Yasaswy wanted to test himself in new terrain, manufacturing.

It was Christmas, but there was work to do. Yasaswy looked up from his notes and told his trusted lieutenants, 'We've been raising money for others. It's time we do so for ourselves.'

The men looked at each other, knowing that when Yasaswy decided, there was already a plan.

'What's the timeline?'

'Before the year ends.' They were about to ask 'fiscal or calendar?', when Yasaswy said, 'Calendar.'

Yasaswy laid down impossible targets, and you didn't argue much with a man of his gravitas. When you set your sights high, unexpected strokes of luck follow. The registrar, known for his rigid adherence to procedure, had gone on extended leave. In his place was an officer with a reputation for pragmatism. Without missing a beat, Siva Ram approached him with the proposal, and they had the company incorporated by the end of the day.

'That's one hurdle down,' Siva Ram muttered.

Yasaswy wasn't satisfied with one company. 'We'll launch two,' he said.

'Like every time?'

'Like every time.'

Within days, two companies were born. Hifco Growth Fund was launched on the last day of 1983, and Hifco Leasing followed on 4 January 1984. Each had a starting capital of one crore. Yasaswy turned to Siva Ram and another colleague, a chartered accountant, P.L. Ananth Ram, to step in as managing directors.

Siva Ram panicked. 'I don't know how to manage this role,' he said. Yasaswy placed a reassuring hand on his shoulder. 'I'm there.' Three decades later, Shah Rukh Khan made the phrase's Hindi equivalent *'Main Hoon Na'* iconic in the eponymous movie.

On his part, Ananth Ram was raring to go. Incidentally, while each of the two companies had its managing director, they operated together functionally. So, Siva Ram invested while Ananth Ram raised money for the two companies.

Initially, both companies were planned as open-ended mutual funds. However, the UTI Act didn't allow that, so the companies morphed into hire-purchase and leasing entities. For Yasaswy, obstacles were opportunities for reinvention.

Meanwhile, R.S.N. Raju, a manager at the Andhra Pradesh State Finance Corporation (APSFC), expressed interest in joining the party. He launched Midland Leasing with a capital of fifty lakh. 'Manufacturing is the future,' he said, planting the seed of an idea in Yasaswy's mind.

Thus, a solvent extraction plant was set up as a division of Midland. And then came Oslin Conductors. The businesses were promising, but the promoters, skilled in finance, lacked the acumen to run them.

Buying into the idea of 'manufacturing', Yasaswy decided to establish a worsted yarn manufacturing project for Hifco Growth. Called Hiflon, the project had loads of ambition but very little groundwork.

Hiflon became Yasaswy's Waterloo.

Brihaspati Vavilala was to oversee the project. Project reports from external sources were dusted off and copy-pasted, even as no one analysed the risks. From a strategy perspective, the business was sandwiched between the supplier and the buyer, between 'raw wool' and 'fabric manufacturers.' The gamble required precision at every step, but enthusiasm outweighed caution.

Enter N.K. Pai, an IIM Calcutta graduate, as the managing director of Hiflon. Pai, used to five-star offices, found himself on unfamiliar ground. Hifco was a start-up in its rawest form, demanding sweat and grind. Disillusioned, Pai left soon.

A couple of hands changed, and then Siva Ram became the overarching head.

Yasaswy chased production. If capacity utilization was twenty-five per cent, he demanded fifty per cent. When it hit fifty per cent, he pushed for seventy-five per cent. Slowly but surely, the team delivered. Each night at 9 p.m., after dinner, Siva Ram would drive down to the Gummadidala factory to take stock of production at midnight, and let Yasaswy know at 9 a.m.

Production scaled up slowly, and soon, it was time to market the product. This is when the next signs of trouble appeared.

The team headed to Mumbai, where the market's most prominent players stayed. 'No one was queuing up to take Hiflon's products,' Siva Ram recalled. 'We had to repeatedly ask for shelf space.'

Just as hopes began to dim, Raymond showed interest. Their executives tested the yarn and found it promising. 'Good strength,' they said. But there was a catch—the actual test lay in how the yarn performed as a finished product.

A few weeks later, Siva Ram was summoned to the Raymond's factory. What he saw there killed him. Piles of fabric sat riddled with imperfections, and the yarn failed when converted to a finished product.

'NEP,' the manager explained, pointing at the flaws.

In the textile business, NEP stands for 'Non-Engineered Particles'—small, unwanted clusters of impurities in textiles. These imperfections, caused during processes like spinning or carding, affect the look and feel of the finished fabric.

For the first time, Hifco realized that they had produced a dud product. 'We'd made yarn that wasn't saleable,' Siva Ram said.

Back at Gummadidala, the team scrambled for answers. After days of research, they learnt that adding anti-static components to spindle surfaces helps. It was an essential oversight, and now, the consequences were showing up.

The company faced a working capital crisis, with money blocked in inventory. Indian Bank, the primary lender, grew restless. It was important to start selling, so Siva Ram flew to Mumbai to knock on every door. Finally, Dhirubhai Ambani's Reliance agreed to buy at a steep discount. Hifco had to accept to keep the company afloat.

It was Yasaswy's first real failure, and he faced it the only way he knew. Head-on.

'We missed the basics,' Yasaswy said quietly.

Soon Midland Leasing also started struggling. And money had to move from Hifco to Midland.

There's always hope for tomorrow. That's the refrain Yasaswy lived by. But Siva Ram couldn't share his optimism. As Managing Director, he was answerable to investors, and the decision to move money out of the company to a group entity began to weigh on him. In 1987, he decided to leave. 'It wasn't an easy decision; it was like walking away from family.'

Yasaswy didn't stop Siva Ram. Instead, he said, 'We'll be your clients.' This was his way of saying that relationships mattered more than roles.

The experience of running the manufacturing units left scars on Yasaswy. Some bets weren't worth placing, no matter how noble the intent. Yasaswy decided never to touch manufacturing again—not even with a barge pole.

The magic had met its meltdown. The man who once raised capital for others now understood what it meant to lose it. Out of that humility would rise his greatest creation: a university built not on profit, but on purpose.

PART II

Building Big

Start where you are. Use what you have.
Do what you can.

—ARTHUR ASHE

Chapter 4

The First Leap

Hyderabad, June 1982

The air in Nagarjuna Hills hung heavy. Inside his modest office, N.J. Yasaswy sat behind a polished mahogany table. The air-conditioner rattled against the afternoon heat. Books overflowed from the cupboards, with some thumbed and others untouched. A framed photograph of his parents rested on a side table. Behind that hung the long frame of Abraham Lincoln.

On his desk lay a book on investments. A colleague had pulled it out from the ASCI library and passed it along. Yasaswy was half-drowsy, flipping through its pages. He had just wrapped up a consulting assignment for a workshop on Security Analysis and Portfolio Management and was sketching out its outline.

Then his eyes froze.

Buried in the appendix was a course outline from the Institute of Chartered Financial Analysts (ICFA), USA. It looked uncannily close to the model he'd been mulling over with Dr Besant Raj and Dr Prasanna Chandra.

For a long moment, he simply stared at the page. Sitting in Hyderabad and reading it felt like a confirmation that he was on the right path. He leaned back and smiled. Outside, thunder rumbled. A fat raindrop smacked the windowpane.

Then another. The sky opened. Within seconds, the city was being washed clean.

Rain had come to Hyderabad. And with it, a spark.

He pushed the chair back, almost knocking into the bookshelf. He didn't waste time.

Reaching across the desk, he picked up the black rotary phone and dialled. He waited for the line to click, tapping his pen against the desk.

Then the voice came over. 'Raj here.'

'A book on investments,'Yasaswy said, skipping pleasantries. 'There's a syllabus in it. It's almost a carbon copy of what we've been discussing.'

'How close?'

'Uncomfortably close.'

He rushed copies to Raj in Chennai and Chandra in Bangalore. Raj read it from cover to cover and called back: 'It's good. We're on the right track.'

Chandra was more surgical. 'It's solid,' he said. 'But it's built for Wall Street. It's too narrow and too focused on capital markets.'

However, Chandra wasn't one to throw out the baby with the bathwater. The American curriculum would serve as the spine. Around it, Chandra would graft modules on corporate finance and financial services, making it relevant to the Indian market. It would be valuable, as India would need analysts, bankers, treasurers, CFOs, and regulators.

This was localization or innovation at its best.

What they didn't have yet was collaboration.Yasaswy drafted a formal letter to ICFA proposing academic arrangements. Weeks passed, and there was no response. That wasn't surprising. In the early 1980s, India was a closed economy. Private initiatives, especially in education, were hardly heard of and India wasn't on anybody's radar.

Two years later, in 1984, during a personal visit, Yasaswy drove three hours from Washington, D.C., to Charlottesville and walked into ICFA unannounced. The reception was polite but perfunctory. There were smiles, handshakes and brochures, but no serious conversation.

He stood before the ICFA building—a world away from Hyderabad, but the dream felt oddly at home.

'They don't see us yet,' he told his colleagues. 'But they will.'

Weeks later, a package landed on his Hyderabad desk. It had ICFA's full curriculum, past question papers, and textbooks. It wasn't a partnership, but it was a crack in the wall.

'Let's build,' he said.

In October 1984, the Institute of Chartered Financial Analysts of India (ICFAI) was incorporated. Yasaswy had it registered under the Andhra Pradesh Societies Act. It was the same year extremists assassinated Mrs Indira Gandhi.

In the decades to come, ICFAI would be known for innovation. But in that moment, it was just a rented office run by a man who refused to wait for permission.

ICFAI now had a name, a logo, and a legal identity.

Next, it needed credibility. That would determine whether ICFAI remained a noble experiment or became a national force.

So Yasaswy assembled a formidable Board of Governors that read like a who's who of Indian finance: LIC's J. Mathan, IDBI's Raghu Raj, UTI's G.S. Patel, and Air India's C.R. Sengupta. Dr Prasanna Chandra came in as the academic architect, and Dr Besant Raj was Chairman. And behind it all was Yasaswy—thirty-something, tireless, and thinking ten moves ahead.

Chandra went to work on the syllabus. The US curriculum was refined, layered with the Indian context, and widened in scope. The result was a course that was capable of training not just analysts but financial leaders.

In August 1985 came the breakthrough.

Alfred C. Morley, the globe-trotting president of ICFA, was on his way to Singapore and dropped by on ICFAI's invitation.

He came. He saw. He was stunned.

He saw stock exchanges older than several American banks and investors quoting the Companies Act from memory. The presence of 4,000 listed companies made his eyes pop up. And the icing was the large army of English-speaking accountants and detailed laws.

When he spoke at IIM Bangalore, the air crackled. Questions flew. It was clear: India was ready. Little wonder that the US institute decided to shake hands.

On 14 August 1985, ICFA and ICFAI signed an MoU, and Morley joined the ICFAI Board. A month later, the Indian CFA programme was launched. When Morley agreed to co-sign the charters with Prasanna Chandra, Yasaswy knew they had won the credibility battle.

It was the legitimacy they needed. Recruiters took note. Students poured in. And slowly, the halo around anything foreign began to reflect on ICFAI.

But every alliance has its expiry date. As India liberalized its economy, throwing open its doors to the world, ICFAI too rewrote its rules. By 1991, ICFAI's curriculum had evolved far beyond the American version. The collaboration ended quietly. ICFAI dropped the borrowed CFA model to build an Indian original. The apprentice had outgrown the master.

A court case on a slightly unrelated matter dragged on until 2007 when the Supreme Court finally ruled in favour of the ICFA.

Yasaswy may have borrowed light from the West but he built a lighthouse for the East. From here, Yasaswy could have paused. He could have coasted. He didn't. Because he was wired differently.

The Relentless Experimenter

By the late 1980s, ICFAI had struck gold with the CFA programme. The finance community had taken notice, and ICFAI was being spoken of in a hushed tone as the 'fourth institute'. You would think Yasaswy would double down on CFA. But no, he was busy sketching his next move.

It was a humid Hyderabad afternoon in 1988, the air heavy with expectation. Inside his small office, Yasaswy's pen tapped against a notepad. He announced that they would be launching a Diploma in Business Finance (DBF) the next quarter.

A colleague coughed. 'Sir, the CFA hasn't even produced a graduating class yet.'

Yasaswy's voice was calm. 'Our mission is not CFA. It's the spread of financial literacy. That's the war we're fighting.'

His argument was simple: finance belonged not just in boardrooms but also on shop floors and kitchen tables. 'What we're doing,' he said, 'is placing finance in every board, every business, every household.'

'Shouldn't we be strong somewhere before we try being weak everywhere?' the colleague ventured.

'That's fair. But if we only invest in certainties, we'll never discover anything truly worthwhile.'

That was Yasaswy's way—a visionary institution builder with the heart of a start-up founder. While others celebrated their triumphs, he was already sketching the blueprint for his next bold experiment. And so began the great diversification drive.

The DBF targeted public fund managers, including IAS officers, PSU executives, and defence staff. The pitch was: 'You manage money. Learn how to do it well.'

The brochures were elegant, and the content was rich. But the audience had no time for five hundred-page textbooks. Dropouts rose, and completion dipped. Looking at the numbers, Yasaswy smiled, wryly. 'We are scaring the market instead of inspiring it. We are selling a Ferrari to someone still learning to cycle,' he said. 'Of course it'll crash.'

ICFAI quickly changed gears. It partnered with undergraduate colleges, offering DBF alongside BCom in small-town colleges. For a while, it worked. But again, students found it hard to meet ICFAI's high standards. The pass rates plummeted, and the brand took a beating.

One evening, a team member nervously brought this to Yasaswy's notice. By sunset, DBF was scaled back. That night, Yasaswy discussed strategic withdrawal. 'If the right product meets the wrong customer, it's the wrong product,' he said.

He reassured his team, 'Sony's first portable audio player was a great idea, but the timing was wrong. That doesn't make it a failure.' Then he added, 'A few years later, the Walkman changed the game.' He was telling them: don't lose heart.

Next came a series of tries.

In 1989, India's stock markets came to life. People started talking about merchant banking. The world of IPOs, underwriting, and issue management was opening. But there was no one to train people to take up that role. ICFAI threw its hat into the ring.

Enter MBFS—Merchant Banking and Financial Services. It was targeted at mid-career finance professionals. But the 1992 stock scam shook the sector, and MBFS limped before being shelved. Next came PFM—Personal Financial Management. 'If we don't teach India's emerging savers how to invest, who will?' Yasaswy said. They even brought SEBI into the conversation. But the Indian saver wasn't yet ready for DIY investing, and PFM found few takers.

Then arrived the CMA Review Programme for Indian students pursuing the US-based Certified Management Accountant designation. India's economic liberalization had made global qualifications an attractive option. However, challenges such as visa restrictions, uncertain career prospects, and a lack of familiarity with international credentials deterred many from embracing the opportunity.

At the post-mortem, Yasaswy remarked, 'Even a perfect seed won't sprout in the wrong season. That doesn't make it useless. It's just...early.'

None of these failures daunted Yasaswy. He launched the Securities Research Centre (SRC), to become the McKinsey of equity research. He hired top talent, invested in infrastructure, and pushed for analyst-grade reports. But the market wasn't ready, and after a few years, Yasaswy called time.

He tried *The Analyst*, a sharp business magazine aimed at capital market readers. It earned praise, but not subscriptions. Eventually, it too faded before rising like the phoenix.

Yasaswy accepted these endings with quiet resolve. 'You don't kill the dream,' he said. 'You just put it to sleep until the market wakes up.'

He wasn't bitter. He believed that even failures left behind scaffolding for future successes.

In 1994, Yasaswy sent his most trusted lieutenant, Subhash Sarnikar, on a five-week global tour—London, New York, and Sydney. The brief was to forge alliances worldwide. Talks with CIMA and CIM in London showed promise, and a Transworld University was floated in the US.

But Indian students didn't buy into the idea. Without job visas, global certifications held little charm.

In 1995, while others were perfecting one campus, Yasaswy did what most would consider madness—he set up nine—not franchises but fully owned campuses. It worked. Over time,

IBS would become ICFAI's crown jewel and the proverbial cash cow.

Later came Tech Schools, Law Schools, and National Colleges, each built with the same stubborn clarity. Not all of them worked. Some soared while others sank. We will talk about each of these later.

Yasaswy wasn't chasing applause. He didn't want to be remembered for a product, but for building an engine of growth. Like Walt Disney, he created a company that could outlive its founder. Like Sony, he hoped ICFAI would be more than any one product. And for that, he turned next to something tougher than innovation—service itself. Not the kind measured by slogans, but the kind felt by every student who walked through its doors.

Chapter 5

Inside the War Room

Yasaswy believed that a great idea was meaningful only if it was flawlessly executed. Now, that belief faced its first real trial.

Ask any CFA, and they'll tell you that 1984 was a sacred year. It was when ICFAI was born; a quiet revolution launched in Hyderabad to redefine financial education in India. But belief isn't enough. Execution is the real exam. That test came two years later.

In October 1986, ICFAI conducted its first exams. A total of 960 candidates signed up. India had not seen a financial exam run like a launch mission. There was no mock exam before launching the real thing, no grandfathering clause, and no honorary recognition for years served in the industry. Everyone—rookie or veteran—had to prove themselves.

Across Dalal Street, a few veterans scoffed: An Indian institute daring to test market analysts? It won't last a season.

From the start, Yasaswy made one thing clear: this wouldn't be an exam that tested memory. It had to test the mindset, judgement, and grit. The format reflected that ambition. It came with three sharp edges. One, MCQs that tricked you into revealing what you didn't know. Two, short answers that tested application rather than recall. And three, long-form essays that called for judgement, not just information.

What candidates didn't see was the war room behind those papers. Each exam paper was prepared by two independent examiners working under one rule: the questions had to be fair but challenging. Once students wrote the exams, the papers were delivered to centralized evaluation camps, where teams read, marked, and debated each answer sheet.

MCQs of course went through computers. But even machines had an internal examiner cross-check every algorithm.

First-time evaluators had every script audited. In the case of veterans, thirty per cent of their papers were randomly re-checked. No revaluations were allowed. There was only one verdict: you passed, or you prepared again. Of course, you could request a detailed performance breakdown, a rarity in Indian academia at the time.

Inside ICFAI, the exam cell ran with the paranoia of a spy agency. Question papers were under lock and key, and result files were triple-checked before release. Yet, beneath the high-pressure systems, there was room for empathy. One year, when a candidate from Abu Dhabi couldn't travel to India to take the exam, ICFAI opened a new centre there. For just one student. It was their version of the Toyota Production System—with every process tracked, every exception flagged, yet, flexible enough to serve thousands of students.

Slowly, the outside world began to notice.

In 1987, Wharton's Marshall Blume delivered ICFAI's Foundation Day lecture. Soon after, Raj, Chandra, and Yasaswy were invited to attend the ICFA (USA) Annual Convention as honoured guests. In a room filled with Wall Street veterans, the three men from Hyderabad stood out. Raj spoke in Taipei. Samikar represented India in Kuala Lumpur. ICFAI joined the global curriculum task force—a clear recognition that they were now part of the big league.

And then, in 1988, ICFAI became a member of the

International Council for Distance Education and joined the International Coordinating Committee, sharing space with the US Financial Analysts Federation, the European Federation, and other global heavyweights.

The bigger shift came at home.

Indian universities began to take note. IGNOU, JNTU, and Bharathidasan started accepting CFA holders for doctoral admissions. It was an endorsement of the programme's credibility. American institutions followed suit. Columbia, Michigan, Cornell, and Kellogg began listing CFA as a valid credential.

Employers opened their wallets.

ICICI, IDBI, IFCI and CRISIL began reimbursing employees who enrolled. So did RBI and NABARD. SEBI, HDFC, and even the Karnataka State Financial Corporation (KSFC) recognized CFA holders for senior roles. SBI agreed to reimburse the full course fee. Stock Holding Corporation, Hyderabad Stock Exchange, and ANZ Grindlays followed.

The signal was clear: ICFAI's rigorous exams, watertight processes, and growing circle of acceptance both in academia and corporate signalled that this was a new centre of gravity.

The foundation had been laid, but keeping people excited require more than global endorsements. As Yasaswy was about to discover, success brings stress. Scale brings cracks.

❦

Novelty has a short shelf life. In the early days, the CFA programme attracted thousands of students drawn by its promise of being rigorous, respected, and accessible from anywhere in the country. Yet, as the months rolled on, many began to falter. There were no classrooms to walk into, no professors to press and provoke, and no classmates to benchmark against. Learning became a lonely journey.

Internal reports painted a sobering picture. Between 1985 and 1993, over twenty-four thousand students enrolled in the CFA programme. Of those, only 237 completed it, a ninety-nine per cent attrition rate. The number stopped everyone in their tracks.

No one spoke. The digits blinked back like an accusation. Yasaswy looked at the data, paused, and said, 'This is a broken promise.'

Suggestions followed. Some were practical, others tentative. Should the programme be made easier? Could they temporarily lower the bar to stem the dropout rate? But Yasaswy held firm. 'We didn't build ICFAI to print certificates,' he said. 'We won't lower the bar. We'll raise the floor.'

It meant raising support systems, not lowering the standards.

So, the team went back to the drawing board. The first idea was to create weekend workshops and refresher classes to give students face time with instructors. It was good on paper, but flopped in reality. A corporate executive who volunteered as an instructor recalled, 'After a ten-hour workday, I'd face ten exhausted faces. It didn't feel like learning.'

By 1992, the team realized that the problem was the delivery model, not the curriculum. There were no scalable tools yet—no Zoom, Coursera, or plug-and-play digital solutions. So, the question shifted: Could ICFAI borrow someone else's classrooms?

The plan was to partner with business schools across the country. ICFAI would provide content, exams, and certification. The schools would offer infrastructure, classroom teaching, and mentoring. The students could pursue both MBA and CFA in one go. Two degrees. One rhythm.

In 1993, fifty-nine business SCHOOLS across India gathered in Hyderabad to hear the proposal. Some came curious, others cautious. But the pitch was compelling. By evening many signed on.

That was the birth of the Multi-Track Instruction Model—part homegrown, part inspired by dual-degree systems abroad. ICFAI had found its scale lever.

Servicing The Customer

Yasaswy endlessly asked himself, 'What does the student need to succeed and to lead?'

From the start, he was clear: 'We are here for the student, not for the staff, not for the system.' That belief was a strategy.

ICFAI wasn't merely offering a course; it was selling 'trust'. And trust, as any brand-builder knows, slips through cracks such as an unanswered call, a delayed response, or a late courier.

So, from Day 1, ICFAI took a decision: treat the student as a customer. In 1986, when PCs were still rare in Indian offices, ICFAI installed one, not for accounts or payroll but for student records. It created its own Management Information System (MIS), monitoring assignments, exams, and student progress long before student Enterprise Resource Planning (ERP) became industry jargon. The same year, ICFAI created a Placement Cell, and sent CVs to over a hundred companies.

Looking back, it was primitive technology. But in its time, it signalled intent.

Once automation arrived, ICFAI committed to responding to student queries within forty-eight hours. They built in-house software with two hundred and fifty coded paragraphs for FAQs. When courier delays crept in, Yasaswy partnered with logistics firms and posted out waybill numbers. Textbooks were to be delivered in seventy-two hours. If the system couldn't do it, it was redesigned.

'If we're not here to solve the hard things, what are we doing?' he would ask. Today, all this sounds like standard SLA. In the late 1980s, it was Amazon-level service.

Over the next few years, a new playbook took shape.

In 1991, ICFAI created another first: academic guides and counsellors in major cities. They were the face of ICFAI in their regions, helping students, answering queries, and even clarifying concepts.

Service was the soul. But a soul needs a system. To serve students well, Yasaswy had to go inside the kitchen.

In the Kitchen

Yasaswy obsessed over details most people didn't even see: a misplaced comma, a misaligned font, or misprinted exam instructions. He believed trust was earned through the small things. He knew that someday he would be gone, but systems would stay. So, he built them to outlast fatigue, memory, and himself.

While the world noticed the glossy ads, Yasaswy stayed in the kitchen—adjusting the flame, perfecting the recipe, making sure nothing burned. He noticed when a phone number in an advertisement was off by a single digit, caught typos in question papers, and flagged missing signatures on student applications.

One day, as he walked past the finance office, he saw a boy standing in line, holding a demand draft.

'What's the queue for?' he asked.

'Fee payment, Sir. Got the demand draft from the bank.'

He nodded and called the accounts head. 'How many students do this every semester?'

'Thousands.'

'And how many banks do we work with?'

'A handful.'

'Then we're the bottleneck.'

Within weeks, ICFAI partnered with over a dozen banks.

Online payments followed soon after. Yasaswy didn't wait for the system to modernize; he just built one that did.

Where others planned in semesters, he measured progress in weeks. At IBS, he meticulously tracked all hundred and four of them—from the initial advertisement to the final handshake at graduation. 'We're not making soap. We're shaping futures,' he reminded his team.

To do that, he built a machine that ran with military precision and a mind that questioned every leak, lag, and loophole. Campus programmes and distance education had separate teams, each with its own marketing, content, delivery, exams, and placement. Branding and examinations, requiring consistency, were centralized, while classroom dynamics needed local nuances and so remained under regional control.

By the early 2000s, every student had a dashboard: 'My Account'. Everything was updated in real time, from dues to courier tracking. Turnaround times were enforced.

He set benchmarks for exams—coverage, clarity, correctness, and creativity. When someone suggested expanding through franchising, he shook his head. 'You can franchise shampoo, not education,' he said. 'This is about a student's future.'

The exam department ran like NASA. Over hundred and sixty question papers were generated every ninety days, sealed in tamper-proof packs, and shipped across the country.

One afternoon, he found three staffers typing marks into a spreadsheet.

By evening, a faculty portal was live. Direct uploads, time-stamped, and acknowledged. Manual entry disappeared by the next quarter.

Every Saturday, Yasaswy studied his dashboard like a flight map.

One day, he pointed to a helpdesk query that had been open for seventeen days.

'Who owns this?' he asked.

'All of us, Sir.'

He shook his head. 'Then no one owns it.'

That night, the team learned that accountability wasn't a department—it was a habit.

By Monday, a new rule was put in place. Every query had to be assigned to a named service officer who was accountable for closing it within a defined time-frame.

When ICFAI sought international accreditation, Yasaswy didn't choose the convenient ones. He picked the hardest: AACSB and EFMD. 'These aren't medals,' he told his colleagues. 'They are mirrors. They show you who you really are.'

He never sought recognition, yet within ICFAI's war room, he commanded like a general—quiet, unassuming, but impeccably precise.

He didn't just think big. He built big. Inside the kitchen, where few looked, he kept the fire alive. In his world, greatness wasn't what you imagined. It was what you executed.

But even the tightest engine needs a loud horn. It was time for the world to see what he had built—boldly, loudly, and unapologetically. From the kitchen to the marketplace, Yasaswy now stepped out, not as a cook, but as the high priest of positioning.

The Priest of Positioning

Yasaswy went beyond promoting a course—he sold. He flung the doors open in a country where higher education was a closed room.

'Certified Financial Analyst,' it said, in bold type, on the front page of the Sunday edition of *The Times of India*.

Positioning isn't about where you stand; it's about the courage to be seen. This was in the 1980s when hospitals and educational institutions didn't advertise. But that was the point. ICFAI wasn't trying to fit in. It was trying to stand out. Harvard didn't put an MBA on the front page of *The New York Times*. Yasaswy did it in India, with none of their legacy and all their daring. Yasaswy turned noise into a mission. No one should ever say they hadn't heard of ICFAI.

Yet, for all the praise it later earned as a marketing powerhouse, ICFAI was born without a market survey or a project report. Maybe that was the only way it could've worked.

In that sense of not doing a survey, it was in good company.

The market doesn't always recognize its needs. Akio Morita didn't ask the world if it wanted a Walkman. Yasaswy didn't ask if India was ready for a course on financial analysis. 'Don't chase demand,' he said. 'Create it.'

There was no formal marketing team in the early days at ICFAI. 'That would only make the rest of us lazy,' he said. Everyone, from academic heads to office clerks, was a marketer. Every pamphlet, every prospectus, and every seminar was a pitch.

'You don't whisper when you start a revolution,' Yasaswy said.

The first ad went live on a Sunday. A few inquiries trickled in. At a meeting two days later, someone hesitantly raised a hand. 'Sir...maybe it didn't work?'

Yasaswy didn't flinch. 'Or maybe,' he said, 'we asked the question on the wrong day.'

Several weeks of examining reader behaviour uncovered an interesting insight. On Sundays, people went straight to the glossy lifestyle sections. On Tuesdays and Fridays, they lingered, read slower, and scanned the whole paper. The next campaign shifted accordingly. This time, the response doubled and, in some places, tripled.

The ads piqued interest. The prospectus, sleek and refined, exuded sophistication. 'Was this flown in from Frankfurt?' one person wondered. The reality was that it came from a printer in Ameerpet. First impressions counted.

Every comma mattered. Once, at a meeting, he stopped mid-sentence. He had spotted a misplaced comma in the new draft. He dialled the printer.

'We'll redo it,' he said.

'Sir, the batch is already out.'

'It doesn't matter.'

To outsiders, it seemed obsessive. To him, a misplaced comma was a crack in the brand wall.

Years later, the world would romanticize Steve Jobs calling a designer at midnight over a pixel. Yasaswy was already calling printers over commas.

The frequency of ads was a learning curve. In the early days, ICFAI ran ads twice a year—in April and in September. Inquiries poured in, then died down. Yasaswy wasn't aiming for spikes; he was looking for rhythm.

So ICFAI tested placements, studied column centimetres, and once even placed an ad next to the editorial page. Finally came front-page solos: very expensive, but immensely effective.

Yasaswy quoted ad guru David Ogilvy, 'You're not advertising to a standing army; you're pitching to a passing parade.' It meant that you had to keep advertising to draw attention.

The first convocation was held in 1989. It was held at the poolside of a five-star hotel. Bugles blared, ushers lined the aisle, and dignitaries took their seats in quiet anticipation.

Starting in 1993, convocations evolved into nationally recognized events covered by the media and attended by top recruiters.

Then came SAP—the Stipendiary Assignment Program. Students became brand ambassadors: they cold-called corporates, sold programmes, and earned commissions. For many, it was their first encounter with sales, their first rejection and their first taste of victory.

'Too commercial,' some faculty members grumbled.

'So is life,' a student shot back.

And then, in the 2000s, Yasaswy pulled out a crumpled map. 'Everyone knows us in Delhi and Bangalore. What about Bilaspur and Jalgaon?' he asked. That began ICFAI's Tier-2 and Tier-3 strategy. The faculty conducted seminars in community halls, not just to sell, but to reassure, listen, and promise.

Years before Starbucks spoke of 'Third Place' towns, Yasaswy sent his team to small towns to open minds.

When it came to pricing many questioned ICFAI's strategy. They said, 'It's outrageous.' When Yasaswy heard it, he countered. 'If it's too cheap, they'll think it's ordinary.'

The programmes came loaded with Harvard case studies and simulations to justify the premium. It wasn't just about paying more. It was about feeling you got more.

Yasaswy didn't just change how education was marketed—he redefined what it meant to market with sincerity. There were no hollow promises. He made advertisements feel like invitations, turned a prospectus into a passport, and never let the brand be just a name; he made it a relationship.

In a world of educators, he was a marketer. In a world of marketers, he was an educator. And somewhere between front-page ads and forgotten street corners, he made ICFAI unforgettable.

But while the world saw the brand, Yasaswy saw the people behind it. Marketing was never the mission—it was merely the invitation. What mattered more was how people felt once they came in. For Yasaswy, the real revolution wasn't in reaching people—it was in what they became after they reached him.

Chapter 6

People, Paisa, and Principles

The real strength behind an institution's rise from good to great lies in an unseen troika—people, profit and principle. Get that troika right, and you can build legacies.

Yasaswy created a culture where people came first, ahead of structure, strategy, or surplus. His credo was simple: 'You don't grow institutions. You grow people. They, in turn, grow the institution.'

ICFAI began lean. Distance learning didn't need armies. A few sharp writers, some backend discipline, and a few fire-starters were enough. The demand for people exploded when ICFAI shifted from correspondence to classrooms. Suddenly, you needed faculty, researchers, marketers, HR, and admissions teams.

During an early hiring round, Yasaswy told a colleague, 'Don't look for someone who wants a job. Look for someone who wants a cause.' CVs poured in. The team scanned for clarity of mind and fire in the belly.

'You can rent a man's brain,' he'd say. 'But his heart must come free.'

At hiring panels, he would toss philosophical questions:

- 'Why do you want to teach?'
- 'Who do you admire?'
- 'What excites you when no one's watching?'

Here's where he truly broke the mould. Most founders build teams to stay, but he built teams knowing they'd leave. 'If your competitors aren't chasing your team member, you've hired the wrong person.'

He built launchpads, not jails. 'Let people rise. Let them shine. And if they flew, bless them.'

That belief shaped a talent pool few institutions could match: bankers, scientists, soldiers, civil servants, MBAs, and mid-career converts.

Yasaswy knew professors weren't moved by pay packages. They were moved by impact. To a new faculty member, he'd say: 'Remember the applause after your first speech? That's what teaching feels like. Every day, day after day.' He was a master motivator. He knew what touched a teacher's pulse, partly because he was once a teacher.

Hiring was Act I, and shaping people was Act II. He expected managers to play coach, not boss, but the coach had to be a taskmaster. Fresh recruits were shown a career path. It was mentorship: raw, real, and one-on-one.

What kept people at ICFAI was the joy of building something bigger than themselves. 'No one pays you to learn to swim,' Yasaswy said. 'You do it because it gives you joy. That's what creating is.'

He built a culture where people chased impossible goals because someone believed they could achieve it. He was fascinated by the Pygmalion Effect—the idea that people rise or fall, based on how you treat them. Treat them like they're world-class, and they'll try to prove you right. Treat them like they're average, and they'll live down to that.

So he bet high. He gave the faculty and campus heads impossible mandates: 'Create this.' 'Launch that.' 'Build a B-school in a Tier-2 city.' Even when they hesitated, he didn't. 'You'll figure it out,' he'd say, and walk away smiling.

Once someone had a mandate, they could pick teams, set budgets, and shape timelines. That leap of faith became a self-fulfilling prophecy.

Take A.V. Vedpuriswar, whom we will meet a little later. He joined the system in the mid-1990s. Yasaswy gave him free rein to teach, lead, experiment, and scale. Before long, Ved was shaping academic delivery, managing research, and guiding a new generation of faculty. 'At ICFAI, you weren't hired to execute someone else's vision,' he said. 'You were hired to create your own.'

Leadership was operational. 'You could walk into Vice Chancellor Subash Sarnikar's office and get a patient hearing,' Ved recalled. 'You'd see Yasaswy from 9 to 6, looking fresh even after a long day.'

Ultimately, Yasaswy didn't just build campuses, he built people. He saw sparks, whereas others saw specs of dust. He raised expectations, and people rose to meet them. He converted ordinary people into restless builders.

But belief alone wasn't enough. Vision needed systems.

'We cannot be a teaching shop,' he declared. 'We have to be a thinking house.' And so, he began where few founders begin—with a library. He called it 'the raw material of a thinking institution.'

Soon, the walls were lined with shelves filled with over 10,000-plus books, journals and international publications. Students could buy books and get reimbursed, while the faculty had access to global databases. Each department had its own mini-library, and heads were asked why they weren't buying more books. It became a haven for readers, writers and restless thinkers.

Then came research. Yasaswy made it easy for a faculty to pursue it. Young associates were hired at decent salaries to do the legwork. The faculty framed the ideas.

He launched a publishing engine: journals, magazines and book series. Submissions were blind-reviewed by external experts. When it came to royalties, the faculty received hundred per cent, while ICFAI received nothing. 'Give them the pride of authorship,' he said. 'They'll give us their best work.'

At first, there was sarcasm. 'Must be nice to have time to write,' a faculty said. Soon one of them got published. Then another. Then, three more. The tone flipped. 'How many have you written this quarter?' was the new coffee-table chatter. Writing became a badge of honour.

He encouraged them to pursue a PhD. 'We'll support it,' he said. A doctoral tag makes you mobile and confident. Let's help you get there.'

A colleague asked, 'What if they get a PhD and leave?'

He countered. 'Imagine if they stayed and didn't grow.'

V.R.K. Chari moved from teaching to building ICFAI's IT wing. Kalyan Debnath turned IBS Calcutta into a placement engine. Rajan Saxena brought in the IIM pedigree. Yasaswy made room for them all.

For years, ICFAI operated from rented spaces and modest buildings. Yasaswy didn't mind. 'Software first,' he'd say. 'Hardware later.' Eventually, though, he changed his mind. 'We need landmarks for the next generation.' He wanted walls that would inspire as much as they enclosed.

Just as he believed in investing in people before property, he believed in earning before expanding. He understood the power of the paisa.

Paisa Power

Looking back, it felt like a script from a movie: the underdog story. Only, this one was real. At the centre of it stood a man who never let money dictate the scale of his dreams.

It was 1984. Yasaswy had just turned thirty-four. He had middle-class savings, not empire-building cash. Yet, he jumped into an audacious ring: education pan-India.

In 1985, ICFAI released its first prospectus. It was priced it at ₹40—a bold move when ₹40 could cover a week's groceries for a young couple. Back then, a freshly minted CA earned about ₹2,500 a month.

But the gamble paid off. The prospectus design was sleek, and the pitch was compelling. With a thirty per cent conversion from prospectus to enrolment, the ₹40 flyer became a self-funding vehicle.

Initially, they had a generous credit line from Imageads, the agency that believed in ICFAI before the world did. Their pockets were politely empty. When Morley visited India, the American institute picked up the tab. Think of it as India's version of a garage start-up: for five years, every rupee was a soldier. And every soldier had to fight.

Then, in 1989, the market changed. The CFA programme's enrolments picked up. Students started coming from Tier-2 towns. Fees nudged upward; and soon a modest surplus appeared.

The real turnaround came two years later.

In 1991, India liberalized, and with that, the stock market caught fire. The timing was poetic. Yasaswy had launched a financial education revolution before the nation knew it needed one. Now, the government was catching up to his vision, and ICFAI, once a fragile boat, caught wind in its sails.

No one would claim that Yasaswy foresaw this, but preparation had met opportunity.

As the stock market ballooned, interest in financial education exploded. Admissions went up, and cash started flowing in. For the first time, ICFAI was awash with money.

Instead of using the cash to buy plush buildings, Yasaswy

raised eyebrows by targeting software. 'Bricks don't teach,' he quipped. 'People and ideas do.' ICFAI continued in rented premises.

ICFAI's distance-learning model was compared to the UK's Open University (OU). But while OU had government backing, the IIMs thrived on state support, Harvard received endowments, and Stanford had venture capitalists. ICFAI had a founder who believed that earned money taught better lessons than donated money.

He didn't see surplus as a celebration. He saw it as freedom. Soon, ICFAI was charging some of the highest fees for distance learning in India. It drew criticism. 'Forty per cent of our respondents said the fees were high,' a staffer once told him.

Yasaswy shot back, 'We're not running a charity. We're funding our and their future.'

You can't subsidize quality forever. So, ICFAI did what any sustainable business must do: it priced cost-plus.

In 1993, ICFAI introduced an instalment payment option. To support it, the institute borrowed from banks against future receivables, relying on student discipline. But then came the defaults. The bank demanded answers. In distress, ICFAI sent legal notices to students, and immediately regretted it.

One student called the office in tears. 'Sir, I'm not refusing to pay,' he pleaded. 'Just…not now.'

The staffer hesitated. There was no policy for emotion.

That evening, Yasaswy called for a review. 'We need a system, not sympathy,' he said. The next week, ICFAI partnered with Canara Bank on a structured education loan scheme.

While ICFAI was building its academic backbone, its Management Development Programmes (MDPs) was going strong. What began in 1986 as modest workshops had, by 1991, evolved into a revenue engine. In 1994, ICFAI booked the Bombay World Trade Center—for the entire year. Eighteen MDPs;

₹12,500 per head for a five-day course. Expensive at the time when that money could buy you a two-wheeler.

But Corporate India didn't flinch. They showed up, and the cheques followed. The MDPs became a silent cash cow.

Yasaswy ran ICFAI like a monk managing a monastery—the scriptures were ledgers, and the miracles were monthly P&L reports.

'We'll rent space, not buy it,' he had declared. By the 2000s, ICFAI operated out of over half a million square feet of leased property. Daily P&L. Daily BRS. Quarterly audits. Inventory records updated live across centres. Mutual fund burns had taught lessons, and so ICFAI parked surpluses in term deposits. Boring, yes. But rock solid.

Someone asked him why ICFAI still ran so tightly even after earning well.

'That's *when* you must be disciplined,' he said. 'Because that's *when* you can grow.'

Even when they slipped—like in 1999, when decentralized interviews backfired, and half the IBS seats went unfilled—he didn't panic. The following year, they reversed the decision, stuck to centralized interviews, and filled the full quota of four hundred and eighty seats.

Soon came a masterstroke: a co-branded card with Andhra Bank—free for students and paid for by ICFAI. The result? Fifty-five thousand new bank customers. Yasaswy smiled.

Today, they call it embedded finance. Yasaswy called it common sense.

Principle: Running with Lights on

If Product was the promise, Process the playbook, Positioning the story, People the spark, and Paisa the power, then Principle was the North Star.

You could copy the courseware and mimic the pricing, but you'd fall short unless you understood the values that drove it. Ultimately, it's not the tallest building that survives; it's the one with the deepest foundation.

For Yasaswy ethics were operational. 'You must run a private institution with public values,' he said. 'That's the only way it'll survive beyond you.'

Every rupee had to be earned, accounted for, and justified. His accountants rejected a reimbursement claim because it included a dinner for 'industry networking.' The note read: 'You were meeting a friend, not an industry.'

Vendors didn't wine and dine with ICFAI staff. 'If you eat at their table, you'll lose your appetite for truth,' Yasaswy warned.

There was a time when ICFAI universities could've minted money through capitation fees. Engineering colleges around them were doing it. Yasaswy didn't. 'The brand isn't the product,' he said. 'The student experience is.'

A young man once walked into ICFAI's Hyderabad office, resumé in hand and hope in his eyes. He also carried a sealed reference letter with a minister's name on top.

The receptionist hesitated but sent the file to Yasaswy's desk. He flipped through it, paused on the seal, and picked up the intercom without a frown: 'Tell him politely that we don't do that here.'

It's a lonely choice in business, especially when the world is busy greasing palms. For him, integrity wasn't a convenient suit. It was his operating system. The values weren't pinned on walls; they appeared in everyday decisions.

Inside the classrooms, the same principle held true. You entered through merit, and you stayed by the rules. Exams were invigilated. Cheating was dealt with swiftly and quietly. 'Cracks in character begin small,' he warned. 'Leave them unchecked; they become fault lines.'

That clarity extended to marketing, too. Once, a regional manager proudly showed enrolment numbers that had doubled. Yasaswy scanned the data.

'How many came through friends and family referrals?'

'Maybe twenty per cent,' the man said. 'We pushed the idea that anyone can get through if they try.'

'Anyone can pass? That's not our philosophy. Fix the messaging.' Then, quieter: 'Selling hope is fine. Selling false hope is betrayal.'

He believed reputations weren't savings accounts you dip into during a crisis.

ICFAI's campuses reflected the man who built them: functional, focused, fuss-free. The money saved went to books, systems, and a good faculty.

Yet, when it came to paying people, he didn't blink. The faculty were paid as per the Pay Commission guidelines, and extra work meant extra pay.

Frugal? Yes. Stingy? Never. Yasaswy once paid a consultant double the agreed fee. 'He gave me more than he had said,' Yasaswy explained. 'Why shouldn't I pay more than I had promised?'

Transparency was a habit. Students could meet evaluators and review their graded papers. Employees knew how they were appraised. Even the no-smoking rule was enforced campus-wide—long before laws required it.

Of all stakeholders, he placed alumni on the pedestal.

With the CFA's regulatory status in flux, credibility outweighed credentials. 'If we falter,' he said, 'our alumni bear the brunt. That's why their voice must be the loudest.'

Each course had a Board, and alumni sat on it. However, Yasaswy warned against groupthink: 'Bring outsiders in, too.'

'Sometimes it takes an outsider to tell you the emperor is naked.'

N.J. Yasaswy could've built empires but he built institutions. Empires make headlines; institutions outlast them. And he didn't run the show in darkness. He ran it with the lights on.

PART III

Trial by Fire

In the middle of difficulty lies opportunity.

—ATTRIBUTED TO ALBERT EINSTEIN

Chapter 7

The Second Curve

It's 1994

India is tasting capitalism for the first time like a kid sipping Coke. It's been three years since Manmohan Singh liberalized the economy.

In Hyderabad, N.J. Yasaswy fears stagnation. Although the CFA programme has been burning bright for ten years, he worries that it is nearing the top of its S-curve. He can feel how students' questions have become repetitive and how the market isn't actually chasing the product.

'Only those who will risk going too far can possibly find out how far one can go,' wrote T.S. Eliot.

Yasaswy leans back in his chair, eyes closed. 'Is this it?' he asks himself. 'Another year of distance learning?' And then, 'What if we stop thinking like a correspondence school and start thinking like a campus?' His alter ego wondered, 'Maybe it is time we bet on fresh graduates?'

These thoughts grew legs and, soon, wings.

The Board decided to offer a full-time PGDBM and tag along the CFA. It wasn't CFA + PGDBM, but PGDBM + CFA. Mathematically, it didn't make a difference, but conceptually, it did. CFA would now play second fiddle.

However, there was one problem: A full-time campus

model would mean real estate, more faculty, unforeseen risk, and the possibility of weakening the brand Yasaswy had spent ten years building.

He floated it as a trial balloon in a meeting with his senior team.

'Why fix what's not broken?' someone ventured. 'Why not scale the CFA instead?' another asked.

He let them finish. Then he smiled. 'A ship that is berthed in the harbour is safe,' he said, 'but that's not what ships are for. Apple was flying high with Apple II, but Jobs still bet the house on Macintosh in 1984. He didn't wait for a crisis to reinvent the future.'

Yasaswy wasn't asking, 'What if we fail?' He was asking, 'What if we never try?'

The idea had a name: ICFAI Business School, IBS, a full-time campus programme. Just as people were beginning to veer towards his thoughts, he felt launching it just in Hyderabad would be too safe and boring. He wanted to launch nine campuses in eight cities.

Dr Prasanna Chandra felt that given Yasaswy's brilliance, 'We could take two or three. Nine was an overstretch.' Dr Besant Raj, ICFAI's calm and cerebral chairman, concurred. Then, recalling their long friendship, he said, 'If anyone can pull this off, it's him,' and signed up.

So in the summer of 1995, nine business schools sprouted: Two in Delhi, and one each in Bombay, Madras, Bangalore, Hyderabad, Ahmedabad, Kolkata, and Pune. It wasn't just bold—it was breathtakingly audacious.

To run this academic scale, Yasaswy handpicked his leaders. Bala Bhaskaran took Ahmedabad. S. Raghupathy reached Chennai. Kalyan Debnath flew to Kolkata. Raj Singh, handled Mehrauli. T.R. Venkatesh chose Bengaluru. V.R.K. Chari managed Hyderabad. Thomas Fernandes and N.K. Jain went to Mumbai and Delhi respectively. Ashok Kumar headed to Pune. Each was chosen not for where he came from but for how he thought—part manager, part missionary. They were all named co-ordinators.

They assembled in Hyderabad for a briefing.

Across the table, a coordinator asked, 'We don't have a national brand or a big campus. Will we get students?'

'We won't get them,' Yasaswy said. 'We'll earn them.' There was silence. Then, one by one, the heads nodded.

A mission had begun.

These were bankers, government officers, pharmaceutical professionals—all with experience in corporate India now set to become academic entrepreneurs.

What made IBS special wasn't just the number of campuses. It was how they worked.

The backend—courseware, systems, structure—was already robust, thanks to ICFAI's distance-learning engine. But how would an MBA programme with zero legacy stand out in a crowded market? That's where Yasaswy flipped the script. He priced the programme at a premium, saying, 'If the price is high, people will think there must be something to it.'

In a world that still hadn't discovered the word 'start-up,' he positioned IBS as a bold brand, not a budget one. It didn't claim to beat the top B-schools – it claimed to fill the massive MBA middle class they'd left behind.

In Chennai, IBS came up in a commercial complex, and 15,000 sq. ft of space was rented. It was the same everywhere. Several students, having graduated from colleges with large campuses found this difficult to digest. But Yasaswy was unfazed. 'This is how US downtown institutes function,' he said.

The B-schools tried to shape how students thought about the world, how they made decisions under pressure, and how they disagreed with grace.

At 8 a.m. in IBS Chennai, a student stumbled in late. The faculty didn't scold. He simply said, 'Six minutes. Convince me why Infosys pays dividends when Microsoft doesn't.' Outside, it was just another Tuesday. Inside, it felt like a boardroom pitch.

Yasaswy insisted that the real world doesn't come with semester breaks. 'We're not running a finishing school,' he said in an early academic review. 'We're preparing them for the trenches.'

The infrastructure wasn't glamorous. The Hyderabad building had more ambition than air conditioning. The computer lab had more heart than hardware. The library was compact but curated. But none of that mattered; purpose replaced polish.

The admissions strategy was clever.

Yasaswy believed in giving everyone a shot. A girl in the 68th percentile was picked because she showed good conversation skills. A full-fledged career counselling and placement team was created in-house, and they built strong relationships with recruiters.

Students were learning how to think, speak and write. They began to stand taller and recruiters took note. Some HR heads dropped in out of curiosity, and a few returned impressed. That was enough. The word spread faster than any advertisement.

By the early 2000s, IBS had become one of the largest business school networks in the country.

For Yasaswy, education was no longer a product—it was an ecosystem. It was the alumni who carried the proof. One was leading a start-up, another had cracked private equity, and a third had quit a plush job to teach kids in Bihar. They didn't all chase the same dream but carried the same courage.

Phadke's Pain

Meanwhile, a bit of an additional backstory needs to be told. It began with a prospectus meant for someone else.

Vivek Phadke, an engineer with BHEL, had no plans of studying finance. A colleague had picked up the CFA brochure and lost interest. 'You might use it,' he had said, handing it to Phadke.

Phadke enrolled, and cleared all three levels at the first attempt.

In 1989, the ICFAI leadership decided to form a twelve-member Board of Governors: six from industry, six from among CFA graduates. It was a move that showed how seriously the Institute viewed its alumni. Phadke was inducted into this Board.

He began by building alumni chapters. At one such event in Bhopal, Yasaswy had come down to address students and the senior management of BHEL. On their way to the airport afterward, they hit a traffic jam. Yasaswy, impatient, suggested they walk the balance distance. But Phadke said: 'Even if we walk, we won't make it. But I'll get you there.'

He pulled strings, and delayed the flight by ten minutes.

That night, his phone rang. 'Come to Hyderabad tomorrow.'

Over lunch, Yasaswy made the offer: 'Join us.'

Phadke joined as Deputy General Manager. It was a time when ICFAI was fluid, entrepreneurial, and agile. If Yasaswy liked an idea, it was approved by lunch and launched by dinner!

Phadke's mandate: expand the CFA programme, build the alumni network, and scale ICFAI's reach.

The turning point came when ICFAI decided to transform the CFA correspondence programme into a full-fledged, campus-based management programme.

ICFAI reached out to the country's top business schools—IIM, XLRI, Goa Institute of Management (GIM), Somaiya, and others—to run the campus-based CFA programme. Initial meetings showed promise. Faculty members even participated in student selections. But then came the pullback.

The core issue was risk. CFA was an external exam. If students trained under their roof failed, the institutions feared reputational damage. One by one, they stepped away.

Yasaswy stayed steadfast. 'We go ahead,' he said.

Phadke led the charge. Leases, faculty, students, classrooms—all in under a week. Six cities were locked in. But Mumbai remained elusive.

One morning, with no breakthrough in sight, he called Yasaswy. 'I've tried everything. I'm coming back.'

Yasaswy said nothing. He simply hung up—a silence louder than words.

Phadke got the message. He cancelled his return flight, opened the city directory and started making cold-calls. One of the calls went to St. Xavier's College.

'Come quickly,' the Principal said. 'I leave for the US tomorrow.'

Phadke explained the situation: IBS had students ready, faculty lined up, classes scheduled—but no venue.

The Principal was firm. 'We have an AC hall but it is booked on various dates.'

'I'll block all remaining dates. If there's a conflict, we'll give leave to students on that day.'

'You're serious?'

Phadke updated Yasaswy who within thirty minutes sent in a Letter of Intent. It was signed that day. Mumbai was secured. IBS Mumbai ran out of Xavier's for two years.

Phadke's tenure saw not only the establishment of IBS but the institutionalization of marketing protocols, entrance exams (IBSAT), and the placement network (IPN).

When ICFAI's degree-granting authority ran into legal

barriers with AICTE, Yasaswy turned to an unconventional solution: create a degree via a registered university in the US. Phadke was sent to Santa Clara, California, to help Sarnikar. For him, it wasn't a trip; it was trust.

But trust, once earned, is not always permanent. Phadke, by temperament, was a rule-bound institutionalist. It made him vulnerable.

The final fracture came over a placement brochure. Phadke had listed senior colleagues as committee members, without naming a chairman. It rubbed people the wrong way. One of them, who expected to be named chairman, took offence. No one raised it directly with Phadke.

Meetings were skipped. Communications broke down. One morning, Phadke was handed a blank piece of paper, and asked to resign.

His father urged him: 'Say sorry. If you want, we'll go together. End this.'

But Phadke wouldn't.

The pain was visible even in the way Phadke recalled it. Not just from being sacked, but from never being heard.

For all their differences, Phadke is unambiguous about what Yasaswy meant to him. 'He was my guru. He taught me how to take risks, how to build, how to back yourself when no one else will.' He admired Yasaswy's risk appetite, obsession with detail, and willingness to pivot.

One image remains seared in his memory.

It was in Auckland, New Zealand, during a conference. Yasaswy had fallen ill with malaria and quarantined. Only Phadke was allowed into the hospital. For four days, he stayed by the bedside. He was caretaker, confidant, and silent witness.

They never spoke of it later. But that silence said what words couldn't—gratitude, regret, and unfinished affection.

The General Who Ran the Rear

Wing Commander R.R. Reddy had no plans of joining academia. After two decades in the Indian Air Force, education wasn't even on the radar. 'I'd taught cadets at the NDA,' he said. 'But teaching is one thing, while running a B School is another.'

Then came a quiet conversation with Yasaswy in March 2000. 'He didn't offer me a job,' Reddy remembers. 'He asked me to serve again.'

'You won't be teaching,' Yasaswy told him. 'We'll hire professors for that. I need someone to run the rear; the logistics, the engine room. We have nine campuses. Do you think you can manage it?'

'Yes,' said Reddy.

Reddy was posted to the IBS Program Coordination Department. Nine campuses. Thousands of students. No manuals. Just expectations. 'It wasn't glamorous,' Reddy recalled. 'But I wasn't here for glamour. I was here to make the machine work.'

Yasaswy preferred defence personnel for a reason. They understand scale and don't blink in a crisis. It was vintage Yasaswy. Bankers taught finance. Industry veterans brought discipline to operations. Entrepreneurs brought energy. Defence officers brought systems.

In his early days, Reddy wasn't included in review meetings. One day, a colleague fell ill. Reddy substituted. The meeting was sharp. On a key issue, Reddy disagreed with Yasaswy.

'I stood up, and said, "Sir, this won't work." Everyone held their breath.'

Yasaswy's face turned red. He paused, thought for a moment, and moved on. From that day, Reddy was invited to every review meeting.

As IBS and ICFAI grew, so did Reddy's mandate. From

academics to examinations to admissions, and then to marketing.

When Reddy took over admissions, the process was patchy with manual records, delayed results, and chaos. Within a year, he had streamlined it, and suddenly, everything ran on time.

Academicians ran the classrooms. But the backbone, viz., operations, the academic calendar, and logistics ran through Reddy's office. It wasn't easy especially when teachers weren't used to the student-first approach.

Student services became Reddy's warfront. Every admission season, hundreds came in, often with missing documentation, some barely scraping eligibility. Parents would plead. Campus heads would protest. 'But we had to uphold process.'

Classroom allotment wasn't random. 'We mixed students by academic background, geography, gender, and marks. All toppers did not go to one section. Engineers and commerce graduates jostled for space. There was an adroit mix of boys and girls. A class had to mirror India,' Reddy smiled. 'By the end of the second month, a Tamil boy and a Jat girl were solving cases together. That was the point.'

Teachers set and evaluated the papers. But the final grades had to pass Reddy's office. By the time Reddy moved on to another department, he had built systems that no longer needed him. Campuses ran like clockwork, admissions were clean, and grading was trusted.

In Yasaswy, Reddy found a commander who walked you to your post, trusted you to hold the line, and never looked back because he knew you would. And somewhere in that quiet trust, an empire learned to breathe on its own.

Chapter 8

The Voices He Built

It was always 10 o'clock. Not earlier, not later.

M.R. Raghu remembers it like clockwork. The morning meetings with Yasaswy, just the two of them. And the Big Man would brew the coffee himself.

That morning, the door opened in the middle of one such meeting, and a teenager, Tejaswy, walked in. 'Dad, I want to go to this place,' he said. 'Can you tell me how?'

Without looking ruffled, Yasaswy calmly gave him detailed directions: which buses to take, where to change, and everything else.

After Tejaswy left, a puzzled Raghu asked, 'But, Sir, that place is just around the corner. Why take such a long route?'

'How else will he fall in love with the city?'

That was classic Yasaswy. Learning had to be through action, not explanation, even if it meant sending his son on a bus ride around the city just to understand its map. This mix of thoughtful parenting and razor-sharp humour was typical of Yasaswy.

That same blend of patience and provocation shaped how he mentored others

Yasaswy never held a doctorate, yet many thought he had a PhD in Economics. He'd laugh it off and say, 'I only learned economics because my wife was writing a paper, and I helped her study.' That was the man—humble and disarming.

The bond between Raghu and Yasaswy started with a leap of faith.

In 1992, Raghu, an internal auditor with the Unit Trust of India (UTI), attended a Management Development Programme (MDP) in Chennai. The speaker: Yasaswy.

'He charmed us,' Raghu says, 'by mixing foreign examples with Indian relevance. He opened windows we didn't know existed.' Only later he would know that this was Yasaswy's signature style.

For Raghu, who came from a modest background, that MDP was an eye-opener. 'As an internal auditor, I was carrying a bag, catching trains, visiting branches, ticking off applications. And here was this man talking about capital markets like they were electric. I thought, 'This is what I want to do.'

During the tea break, Raghu approached him—nervous but determined. 'Sir, I work in the public sector. But my heart's in research and investments. Can you help me make a shift?'

'Come see me when you're in Hyderabad.'

The following week, Raghu took the Charminar Express, reached Yasaswy's office, and walked in.

'You came all the way here just to see me?' Yasaswy asked, taken aback.

'You told me to.'

Yasaswy laughed. 'I told you to see me whenever you are in Hyderabad, not to come here only to see me! Ok. Join me as a research analyst.'

And just like that, Raghu left a government job to join an unknown entity. 'My father-in-law thought I'd lost it.' But somewhere deep down, I knew I was chasing a life I wanted.'

Over the next few years, Raghu saw every shade of the man—the demanding boss, the strategic mind, the comic genius.

One of their most significant initiatives was setting up the

Security Research Centre (SRC). 'At one point, we had thirty analysts covering listed companies. We produced independent research reports—not broker-backed, but purely educational and analytical.'

The model was novel and brilliant: recruit interns from IIMs, XLRI, and top institutes—about two hundred of them, year after year—bring them to Hyderabad, house them for a week, train them rigorously in equity research, then send them to the field for company analysis. They would return, write reports, and submit them.

'And they loved it,' Raghu says. 'Even today, some of them reach out to say how that one summer shaped their careers.'

Alongside these projects, Yasaswy's strict discipline showed in many ways.

Raghu recalls a Faculty Development Programme (FDP) for college principals. 'About a hundred were expected. The agenda set a 10 a.m. start. By 10, only fifteen had turned up.'

Yasaswy stood up, welcomed the fifteen, and began his session.

Those who came late were told to go back and return the next day.

'They were furious,' Raghu recalls. 'These were college principals. But the next morning, by 9.50, every seat was filled. Yasaswy's lesson on punctuality was silent, unwavering and unforgettable.

Despite being a stickler for discipline, he had a huge humorous side to him. Raghu recalls being overwhelmed one day and struggling to find good analysts. During their 10 a.m. meeting, he expressed his concern and asked how to get ten of them within a week.

Yasaswy adjusted himself in the chair as if about to make a serious suggestion.

'You know Panjagutta police station?' he asked.

'Yes.'

'Tomorrow, go there at 4 a.m. Lorries come to pick up daily labourers. Pick two or three of them. Bring them here.'

Raghu blinked.

'If you want people by tomorrow, that's your option. You'll have to wait a few months if you want good analysts.' He delivered it deadpan. The humour would hit you a moment later.

To Yasaswy, mentorship wasn't about teaching answers but provoking better questions.

But Yasaswy wasn't just funny or firm. He was deeply strategic.

'Before every meeting with a corporate honcho—be it from SEBI, RBI, anywhere—he'd coach me,' Raghu says. 'He told me: never ask for three things from a decision-maker. Ask for just one. He'll pick the easiest and leave the rest if you ask three. But if you ask just one, he must choose between yes and no.'

That defined Yasaswy's approach: clear, sharp and strategic.

Another day, Yasaswy said, 'You're meeting SBI, right?'

'Yes, Sir. But they are a large institution.'

'Remember, there is no such thing as an institution. Behind every institution, there's just one guy. Find him. Shake his hand. Win his trust.'

Raghu also carried another advice into every meeting with regulators, government officials, and giants of Indian industry: Don't get overwhelmed by the boardroom table. Look for the human being behind the title.

That clarity, that razor-sharp way of cutting through the noise, was one of Yasaswy's greatest gifts.

Of course, identifying the right person was only half the game. The other half was to make your pitch count.

'You get five minutes. Make it powerful. Give them

context, prove your worth, and earn the next twenty minutes,' Yasaswy said. 'If you can't do that, the name on your visiting card won't help you.'

From sending his son on a winding bus ride to teaching principals punctuality the hard way, from building a cutting-edge research centre to crafting jokes with a straight face—Yasaswy left an imprint that was in equal parts wisdom, wit and willpower.

Raghu smiles and says, 'I've seen all sides of the man. He was unpredictable, intense, funny and generous. But always, always, he meant what he said.'

In a world that often spoke louder than it acted, Yasaswy practised what he preached.

In 1995, an MDP was taking place in Mumbai. It was a high-profile event attended by research analysts and fund managers.

Yasaswy delivered the keynote, and as usual, it was crisp and insightful. What followed were sessions by guest speakers, including top academics like Krishna Palepu and R.Vaidyanathan. Raghu would handle portfolio management; Krishna Mohan, a colleague and a technical analysis expert, would talk about charts.

That day, a senior professor arrived late. He was unprepared, and it showed. His talk was vague, filled with academic jargon, and wholly disconnected from the hands-on world of fund managers.

The session bombed. Raghu, who followed him, had prepared well. His session shone.

Back in Hyderabad, Yasaswy said, 'Tejaswy told me your session was the best. Do you know why?'

'I prepared well, Sir.'

'Good. Never go anywhere unprepared.'

It wasn't just praise; it was recognition. And a reminder. Yasaswy hated unpreparedness. Whether you were a professor or a finance minister, it didn't matter. If you showed up unprepared, he would call it out.

❧

Sometimes, it wasn't in the boardroom or classroom that Yasaswy revealed his core. It was in moments no one expected.

Raghu remembers an Air India flight to Mumbai. Yasaswy was in the aisle seat, and Raghu was beside him. Across the aisle, a mother wrestled with a restless toddler. Coffee spilled, and a hostess, visibly agitated, raised her voice at the young mother.

The cabin watched silently. No one intervened except Yasaswy.

When the hostess returned with the coffee tray, Yasaswy took the tray from her hands.

'No coffee will be served until you apologize to that lady,' he said.

She resisted, then firmly declined, insisting it wasn't her fault.

Yasaswy would have none of it. 'Remember, we are paying your salary. Call your manager,' he said, calm but resolute.

Only after the air hostess and manager apologized to the woman did Yasaswy return the tray.

'It wasn't drama,' Raghu says, 'Everyone on that flight saw what standing up looks like. It was something he expected from every leader he mentored.'

❧

'Subscribe to *The Economist*—on your own,' Yasaswy once told Raghu. 'If the company gets it for you, it'll land on your desk, pile up, and gather dust. But if you buy it, you'll read it.'

Raghu remembers how that statement stunned him. It wasn't about a magazine. It was about investing in your own growth. Yasaswy deeply believed that knowledge pursued personally stuck far better than knowledge handed down.

One day, Raghu got an offer from the Indian Bank Mutual Fund in Chennai. 'It was a perfect fit—my domain, my city. I was ready to return.'

When he broke the news to Yasaswy, the reply wasn't what he expected. 'That's good,' Yasaswy said. 'But I have something better.'

He revealed plans for a Securities Research Centre (SRC), and offered Raghu the opportunity to head it. He pulled out a blank sheet of paper and handed it over. 'Write what you want.'

No negotiation. Just trust and respect.

'That,' Raghu says, 'was magic.'

Raghu accepted. By mid-1994, SRC was launched, and the dream ran wild for a while. Capital market research, high-calibre analysts, and partnerships with top institutions. SRC was bold, fast, and idealistic. Still, even great ideas meet resistance in the real world.

In the India of 1990s, equity research didn't sell. Brokers gave free advice. Fund managers had in-house teams. When SRC didn't yield returns, Yasaswy cut the cord. He didn't show him the door, but offered Raghu a transition. 'Take charge as Dean of IBS Tilak Nagar for six months,' he said.

Raghu took it, knowing that he was not cut for it. His heart was in research and investment. Slowly, he wound his way to the Middle East. In letting him go, Yasaswy showed that endings could be graceful.

Even after Raghu moved abroad, the two stayed in touch. The business didn't work, but the bond remained.

Yasaswy was a strategist to the bone. And for those who worked closely with him, he was a leader with uncanny clarity. He'd walk in at review meetings with a calm face and surgical clarity, agenda in hand, fully prepared.

'And he would talk about your department,' Raghu recalls,

'as if he had been sitting next to you daily. Even though he had ten other departments to worry about.'

No micromanagement. No interference. Just focused on value addition.

'He encouraged you to hire more intelligent people. "Don't fear control," he'd say. "Hire people smarter than you. It'll make your life easier."'

And yet, for all the structure and speed, he retained warmth. Yasaswy was a conversationalist who used charm and curiosity as his sharpest tools. He also knew when to pull out.

For six years, Raghu worked alongside him. Yasaswy trusted his team, but he ran a tight ship. But in that time, those 10 a.m. meetings became more than routine; they became lessons in life.

The Magazine He Didn't Read

While Raghu was running SRC, another experiment was brewing just a few feet away—quieter and more accidental. *The Analyst* was born out of a desire to create a voice to participate in national conversations.

Sanjeev Varma was in Hyderabad on a personal break, waiting outside his sister's office, when Yasaswy paused mid-step, and said, 'Come in. Let's have some tea.'

The invitation was casual, but the conversation was not. Yasaswy spoke about work, ideas, and the economy and, somewhere along the way, said almost casually, 'We're starting a magazine. Want to help build it?'

Sanjeev hesitated. 'I've never worked in publishing. I've no background in journalism.'

Yasaswy smiled. 'Neither do we. We'll figure it out.'

And that's how *The Analyst* was born in the office of a man who believed possibility was more important than preparation. It wasn't entrusted to an experienced editor but to someone trained in rural management. Sanjeev agreed because he had no other offers on the table.

The magazine started small—more an in-house journal for a captive audience. But Yasaswy wanted it on the newsstands, carving out a space for itself; loud, proud, and unapologetic. It would be distinct from the business and investment magazines, in that it would educate and help readers make sense of the financial markets.

'We'll launch big,' he said.

'How big?' asked Sanjeev, half-expecting restraint.

'Full-page ad. *The Times of India*.'

'Who's designing it?'

'We are.'

There was no agency. Just Yasaswy, Sanjeev, and a designer. Here's how the first ad came off.

A whiteboard leaned against the wall. A4 sheets lay scattered on the floor, one with 'Decoding Business' scribbled in red.

'Too dry,' Yasaswy muttered.

Sanjeev circled it. 'What about "India's New Business Voice"?'

'We're close,' Yasaswy said. 'But not there yet.'

That night, they rejected twelve taglines and one pizza. By morning, they had their ad. Every word and visual was crafted in-house, not out of thrift but pride.

Soon, the team grew. Writers, illustrators, marketers began trickling in, mostly young, untested and unafraid. At its peak, *The Analyst* had a dozen writers from diverse academic backgrounds—MBAs, BTechs, post-graduates and aspiring CAs—who shared a common goal to demystify the world of finance, and all running on Yasaswy's impossible pace.

There were no warm-ups. You jumped in, found your footing mid-race, and kept going. Yasaswy delegated with a smile and left you standing at the deep end. To outsiders, it looked chaotic; to Yasaswy, it was choreography.

One afternoon, he called Sanjeev and said, 'Let's launch a diploma in capital markets.'

After what appeared to be an eternity, Sanjeev found his voice. 'But I run a magazine.'

'Now you also run a diploma.'

'I've never written courseware.'

'You won't write it at all. But you'll lead the team that does.'

There was no option to do dry runs and then decide. You were either in or out. And once you said yes, Yasaswy made you believe you could do it, even when you weren't sure.

'I honestly didn't know I had the potential,' Sanjeev would later say.

As the magazine matured, the demands multiplied.

The Analyst wasn't just about content. It was a tool, a megaphone, a brand vehicle. Yasaswy used it to create public visibility through events, panels, and awards. They were credible, tightly curated, and backed by intellectuals like Dr Prasanna Chandra.

When funds ran short for an event at the Taj, Sanjeev flew down to Mumbai and convinced the LIC chairman to underwrite a ₹5-lakh sponsorship. It was a fifteen-minute meeting where conviction sold faster than any proposal.

When he thought he'd earned a breather, another curveball came flying.

'The Asian Securities Analysts Federation's Conference is coming to India,' Yasaswy announced one morning.

'Fantastic,' said Sanjeev. 'Who's handling our end?'

'You are.'

It took every ounce of self-restraint for Sanjeev not to fall off his chair. He had never run an event of that magnitude—dozens of speakers, hundreds of delegates, a global audience. But Yasaswy didn't wait for readiness.

He declared the race started and trusted you to find your stride.

There are moments when a glossy cover can't hide the hollowness inside. For Sanjeev Varma, that moment came shortly after he joined the ICFAI and flipped through an issue of the CFA Journal that was planned to be launched on the stands. And he was in for extreme disappointment.

'The writing was weak, the grammar was off, and the thinking was scattered all over the place,' he admitted later. 'It felt like a college newsletter, not a potential business magazine.'

Next morning, coffee cups in hand, the team gathered in Sanjeev's cramped cabin. For the next eight hours, they dissected the journal line by line. Every headline, every caption, every argument was put under the microscope. 'Looking back, I have to tell that the learn-as-you-go journey was difficult and yet richly rewarding for all of us. We later called it the "Thousand Errors" meeting,' Sanjeev recalled.

What shook him wasn't just the quality. It was the realization that the team expected to deliver a national-grade publication had no formal training. Few had studied journalism, and fewer understood the craft of storytelling. There were exceptions. Aarati Krishnan, who would go on to edit *The Hindu Business Line*. S. Sridhar, who would pivot into finance and portfolio management. But for most, writing was a task, not a talent.

And yet, through it all, Yasaswy never interfered.

'He gave us full freedom,' Sanjeev said. 'Not once did he ask what the lead story was or what theme we were running.'

That silence was telling. Yasaswy's gaze was elsewhere. Advertising, distribution, revenue, and brand visibility. For him, in this case, the product was a bridge, not a destination.

That freedom came with its risks.

A senior adman took issue with a line in the promotional ad, and Yasaswy wasted no time calling Sanjeev in. His tone carried an unusual chill.

'You should've run this past someone,' he said.

Sanjeev nodded. But who was there to run it past? No editorial board, no second pair of eyes. Just a founder moving faster than anyone else. That story didn't end with *The Analyst.* The same pattern played out across other ventures—velocity over vetting.

Then came another pivot—Transworld University, an attempt to leverage the foreign degree craze sweeping across India. The model was part-US, part-Hyderabad, and Sanjeev Varma was, again, handed a fresh hat.

'Suddenly, I was teaching Strategic Management,' he said.

Each week brought a new role. One day, a professor; another day, an editor; a third day, a salesman, and occasionally, an event organizer.

'Yasaswy used to say, "We're all actors, and must give our best performance in that moment"' Sanjeev recalled with a smile. 'But the problem is that if you keep acting, you stop mastering anything.'

There was no shortage of ideas, but often, they outpaced planning. Even when respected voices on the Board like Dr Chandra or Dr Raj raised flags, they were overruled. 'If you didn't agree, you were steamrolled.' It was not out of ego, but out of urgency. It wasn't malice, but momentum. And sometimes, it left bruises.

Once at a Board meeting Dr Raj looked at Yasaswy and said, 'Let Sanjeev take some time off. Woo a girl. Get married.'

Yasaswy grinned, 'Sanjeev is smart enough to make the time without taking time off.'

The man could be brutal and unrelenting. Yet somehow, even when overworked or underprepared, the team stayed, not for the structure but for the spark.

That spark, the force that transformed engineers into writers, was both Yasaswy's gift and his burden. They called it madness, but it moved mountains.

Even after Sanjeev moved on—first to consulting with Satyam, and later to Nokia—the relationship endured. There were catch-up calls and shared stories.

So, how were his latter-day bosses? 'Well, they would plan for a year. As for Yasaswy, he'd think of it yesterday and launch it today.' Some bets failed. But he accepted failure without drama, without shame. For him, momentum was a way of keeping the institute from falling asleep.

Chapter 9

Ink and Intention

Long before the business schools, there was the writer.

It began with a cheque. Rupees forty for a well-written book, *Finance for Non-Finance Executives*. The moment wasn't about the money. It was about being read.

For N.J. Yasaswy, that cheque was proof that knowledge could transcend borders. He wanted to make financial wisdom accessible to everyone, long before it became a catchphrase.

'He wasn't after fame,' said E.A. Srinivas, who first met him in the 1970s. 'He was trying to build something of value.' Yasaswy wrote in a style that demystified the magic of money and together, the duo started a page in *The Hindu* titled 'Finance and Family'.

Buoyed by the response, he began writing more. That's how the book *Finance for Non-Finance Executives* came about. It was based on the course he taught at ASCI. Kapil Malhotra stood behind many of Yasaswy's books, but their journey together didn't begin with a pitch; it began with a letter. While at Vision Books, Kapil reached out, suggesting Yasaswy publish with them. What moved Yasaswy to say yes, we may never know. But what followed was the start of a lifelong friendship.

Many other publishers approached him later, but he politely declined. 'That kind of loyalty,' Kapil said, 'is rare today.'

Yasaswy took the written word seriously, believing it could

simplify knowledge and open doors. But his faith in writing didn't stop at finance.

❧

His reverence for the written word wasn't confined to books; it stretched into languages, with special devotion to Telugu. It bothered him that many Telugu children couldn't read the script anymore. ICFAI's academic head, G.R.K. Murty, arranged a meeting between Yasaswy and Prof. S.S. Prabhakar Rao, who had just proposed an English Studies journal. They expected the conversation to revolve around English. Instead, it veered towards Telugu.

Yasaswy spoke about Vemana and Baddena—Telugu poets whose words once lit up households but were now slipping out of reach. He wanted to do something about it. That afternoon, the C.P. Brown Academy was born.

Its mission was ambitious—bridging classical Telugu with modern learners, particularly those schooled in English. Yasaswy envisioned an unconventional approach: teaching the Telugu alphabet through the Roman script. He wanted monographs on under-recognized Telugu icons such as Durgabai Deshmukh, Y. Nayudamma, Rayaprolu Subba Rao, etc. He pushed for translations of Allasani Peddana's *Manu Charitra*, and the five great Telugu epics.

Rao remembered how relentless Yasaswy was. 'His mind was ever fertile with new ideas. It was quite a job for lesser mortals to keep pace with his speed.'

Even his approach to building advisory teams had a touch of wit. On one occasion, Rao presented a list of scholars, omitting his wife, Dr S. Padmavati. When questioned, he quipped, 'She's my wife.'

Yasaswy smiled. 'That isn't a disqualification.'

He didn't just fund ideas. He followed through.

Rao arrived with a few notes at one meeting to discuss a *Shakespeare and Management* course. Yasaswy came with a stack of books and a dozen insights. 'That thoroughness,' Rao said, 'marked him apart.'

❧

Prof. C. Subbarao had a similar story.

One day, the retired English professor received a call. It was Yasaswy, asking if he could translate Shakespeare's Sonnets into Telugu—not for vanity, but to introduce timeless literature to new readers.

Later, when the project was halfway done, Yasaswy called again. This time, it was Gandhi. Joseph J. Doke's *M.K. Gandhi: An Indian Patriot in South Africa* (2006) was to be translated into Telugu.

'Boy, did I feel privileged,' said Subbarao.

The only time the two met was at the Telugu Bharathi Award function. Yasaswy had instituted it under the C.P. Brown Academy with a cash prize of ₹2.5 lakh and a gold medal. The award was given annually to a distinguished writer for his outstanding contribution to Telugu.

Subbarao arrived early and spotted a slightly stout man with luminous eyes seated in the back row. That, he guessed, had to be Yasaswy. And it was. He stood apart not by position but by presence.

After the event, as the audience trickled out, Subbarao walked up and introduced himself.

'A CA once told me you could have won a Nobel if you had pursued research.'

Yasaswy laughed. 'Don't believe such stories.'

Subbarao added, 'Your presence is striking.'

'All bald men look bright in the light.'

That was Yasaswy—humble, funny, and always in control.

His mission wasn't academic. It was cultural. He believed India's rich textual traditions, in any language or discipline, should be made usable, teachable, and shareable.

Even as the Academy took root, another front opened—the printed word itself. Yasaswy was now thinking beyond language preservation, towards the machinery of publication and reach.

G.R.K. Murty, a former banker-turned-educator, passed by Yasaswy's cabin one night. He found him studying transparencies for a presentation scheduled the next morning.

Each slide. Each word. Read with the intensity of a first-time speaker. Murty watched, realizing this was not rehearsal; it was devotion.

'That was when I realized,' Murty said, 'he wasn't just a leader. He was a storyteller. He thrived at the leading edge of innovation.'

That same obsession with quality birthed the ICFAI University Press—an audacious initiative to run twenty-seven journals across disciplines, published monthly and delivered to thousands of subscribers. It gave faculty nationwide a platform to write, reflect, and be read.

Yasaswy wasn't hands-off.

He tracked research across disciplines, cited international publications in faculty meetings, and nudged teams to revise content for rigour and relevance. He read the journals himself, offered feedback, attended editorial design meetings, and constantly reminded his team: 'Global standard. Indian reality.'

Under his guidance, the ICFAI University Press flourished.

Some initiatives faltered, some journals folded up, and some dreams had to be shelved. For Yasaswy, these were parts of his larger mission. He quickly neutralized potential risks before they could spiral out of control.

He did it with dignity when a division had to be shut down.

'Let's support the people who must move out,' he said once. 'He has school-going children. Let's help him adapt.'

By then, the circle had closed. What began with a single book and a borrowed typewriter had now become a publishing ecosystem—from newspapers to monographs, journals to university presses.

A cheque. A letter. A monograph. A sonnet. A speech. Srinivas remembered the thrill of that first cheque. Malhotra, the loyalty. Rao, the breathless ideas. Subbarao, the humility. And Murty, the fire behind the slides. They all said the same thing: Yasaswy saw words as more than language. He saw them as instruments to include, to inspire, to build, and to uplift.

For all his accomplishments, he remained grounded. 'He lived a life,' E.A. Srinivas said, 'that danced in the shadow of greatness.'

Chapter 10

Unidentical Twins

ICFAI National College (INC) and Magnus School of Business (MSB) had the same parentage. They were unidentical twins. One was presented with pride, while the other was publicly orphaned and privately supported. Few understood this sleight of strategy, and which is why the story must be told.

A map hung on Yasaswy's office wall. Small, coloured pins were stuck across places most people flew over—Bilaspur, Dharwad, Guntur, etc. Towns where no one expected a B-School to bloom.

'These are opportunities,' he said, tapping gently. The 'opportunity' matured into ICFAI National College (INC), carrying Yasaswy's vision forward.

By the early 2000s, India's IIMs took pride in accepting the top 0.1%, and private B-schools marketed their exclusivity like a badge of honour. What about the millions of small-town kids who couldn't cough up ₹10 lakh for a two-year MBA? In 2003, that's where INC marched in.

Yasaswy called it 'retail education' and was proud of it. He wanted education to reach not just metros, but mofussil dreams. The format was meant for wide distribution. The goal wasn't to build one iconic institution but to seed a hundred, then two hundred.

And he did it. At one point, INC spread to 170 towns—

from Kottayam to Kanker. Compared to IBS, it had different fees and geographies, but it wore the same DNA regarding rigour, reach, and relevance.

Yasaswy didn't just expand education; he industrialized learning without stripping it of its soul.

Each campus ran like a lean startup: five to twelve faculty, eighty to two hundred students, a 10,000 sq. ft space with classrooms, soft-skills labs, a small library, and big dreams. The faculty were recruited locally and trained centrally in Hyderabad.

INC's idea was to flood the market with competent managers. It was a grounded, no-frills answer to India's managerial hunger. The boys and girls were first-generation learners—quiet kids from semi-English schools, some of whom didn't even own a pair of formal shoes. A student in Rajahmundry still recalls how his father pawned his scooter to pay the first fee instalment. When he landed his first job in Chennai, the family celebrated.

Yasaswy read the weekly reports, reviewed placement numbers, and tracked faculty feedback. His fingerprints were everywhere.

If IBS was about polishing diamonds, INC was about mining them. So, what made INC tick?

For starters, INC didn't wait for students to come. It went out and found them. Session by session, seminar by seminar. 'Here's what a business career could look like,' they'd say. 'Here's how case studies work.' They'd run them through slides and mock interviews.

Then, the troubles began. By 2005, the regulatory weather got hot.

The Supreme Court's verdict on *Prof. Yashpal vs. State of Chhattisgarh* raised questions about the jurisdiction of private universities. The UGC and AICTE began asserting themselves.

Public interest litigations landed in courtrooms from Delhi to Chennai. Suddenly, scale was not admired, but interrogated. The questions weren't about quality but legality. Who authorized these degrees? Under what jurisdiction do they come?

Yasaswy read the signals, sensed the sentiment, and decided. 'If we can't run it clearly, we won't run it at all.'

In 2009, INC stopped new admissions nationwide. There were no half-done batches. Every student was supported to the finish—classes held, internships completed, and final placements delivered. The last cohort graduated in 2010.

It was INC's final lesson: how to exit with integrity.

More than 35,000 alumni and 4,000 trained faculty went through the INC portals and left a mindset behind. Their resumes show that you didn't have to be from a metro to make it in management.

The Colombo Gambit

N.J. Yasaswy flipped through a stack of resumés, eyes scanning with practised speed. He wasn't looking for qualifications; he was looking for people who could build without being told how.

That's when he saw it.

Colonel. Artillery. Instructor in Gunnery. MBA, MSc Tech in Weapon Systems. Served during Kashmir militancy at its worst and also through the Bombay riots.

He glanced up and told his registrar, E.N. Murthy, 'Let's call him in.'

That resumé belonged to Col. Sukumaran, a recently retired Army officer in his late forties.

Yasaswy was laying the ground for something audacious—a college in every district of India. And to do that, he needed people who could execute with precision, intelligence, and unshakable ethics.

One morning, two men—R. Prasad, an IIT-IIM graduate, and Col. Sukumaran—met Yasaswy at his office.

There was no preamble. Yasaswy simply said: 'I want to build a management college in every district of India.'

Google said, 'India has five hundred and eighty-five districts.' So it was five hundred and eighty-five colleges. When they stepped out, Prasad told the Colonel, 'Feels like we've been asked to climb the Everest.'

That's how Yasaswy operated. 'He simply set the bar, and let you figure out the ladder.'

The first milestone was thirty-five colleges in Year One. He left the 'how' to his generals. Prasad would lead academics, including faculty recruitment. Sukumaran was tasked with infrastructure, logistics, and administration. They began with ads, identified local leaders to head each college, and brought them all to Hyderabad for training. They also visited shortlisted premises and took calls on each.

Twenty-six campuses were launched in the first year. The fee was set at ₹105,000. Sukumaran visited every college, speaking to parents, earning their trust. With INC headquarters established, Marketing, Student Services, Examinations, Training & Development, Legal, HR and other departments were set up. It looked less like a college network and more like a military command centre for learning.

The following year, they launched a national entrance exam. Numbers surged. Within three years, INC had broken even and had a surplus. That was Yasaswy's formula: scale with soul, speed with substance.

At its peak, there were one hundred and seventy-three ICFAI National Colleges.

Another morning, Yasaswy called Sukumaran into his room.

'We're planning to start a college in Sri Lanka—Colombo. Would you like to lead it?'

Sukumaran didn't even hold a passport. But he said yes.

Within four days, passports and clearances were arranged. Sukumaran flew to Colombo with Padmanabhan (Paddy) Nair, an IIM Ahmedabad graduate who did his school education in Sri Lanka, because his father had once served as India's High Commissioner to Sri Lanka.

It was tense. The LTTE was still active. Sukumaran's army background raised flags at checkpoints, but they pressed on. The streets were lined with sandbags and caution, but so were they with hope.

They met Nirupama Rao, then India's High Commissioner to Sri Lanka for the occasional support. She was sceptical, until Paddy pointed to her his father's name appearing on the board listing High Commissioners. She also saw the proposal's seriousness. Her support turned the tide.

An advertisement was placed, and on the same day, a campus site was frozen. Sukumaran faxed the pictures to Yasaswy. Within hours, approval was granted with advance payment released. No committees. Just a leader who trusted you to do the job. That trust became the real currency of the ICFAI movement.

Peter Woodman, a retired Group Captain and an ace pilot, was appointed Principal. The inauguration took place on the lawns of the Taj Samudra. Dr Panduranga Rao, Prof. P.V. Indiresan, then Director, IIT Delhi, and Lakshman Kadirgamar, Sri Lanka's then foreign minister, attended. Kadirgamar would later be assassinated.

The Sri Lanka campus thrived. Students chose it over nearby British institutions. Degrees were awarded through ICFAI Tripura.

What made INC different was both scale and intent. Yasaswy understood that most students in small-town India wanted jobs. He built INC for them.

Job-oriented curriculum, practical delivery, strong placement cells—it was a working-class MBA for an ambitious India, and one that didn't compromise on quality.

Sukumaran recalls a campus visit in Goa: 'Yasaswy sat on a bench, chatting with the faculty and admin staff. They were stunned. The Big Boss himself sitting casually.'

'We never hired agents to recruit students or faculty,' Sukumaran said. 'And that shocked people.' ICFAI was playing by different rules, and that earned it loyalty from students and hostility from competitors.

To manage scale, regional offices (RO) were set up. Later, these ROs were brought under zonal offices (ZO), with regional and zonal heads taking care of the colleges under their respective areas. The model was maturing. It was a spoke-and-wheel arrangement modelled after the defence forces. Education had never been organised with such military clarity.

Then began the legal troubles.

A Supreme Court judgement blurred the line between degrees and diplomas, triggering panic among students and parents. Yasaswy moved fast. His team offered transfers to ICFAI Dehradun, which had university status. But uncertainty stung, and admissions fell.

The closure was announced at Pragati Resorts. Sukumaran still remembers the stunned silence in the room of principals.

Later, sixty-five campuses were sold to Everonn, the Chennai-based educational entity. Staff retained jobs, landlords got their deposits back. Financial chaos was avoided. It was another show of Yasaswy's belief in dignity, even during a shutdown.

Of Yasaswy, Sukumaran said, 'He was a real teacher. He explained, he empowered, and he solved. He made you feel seen.'

He recalled one Saturday when crores had to be refunded to parents the next day, a Sunday. 'I called him. He just said,

"You'll get the money." We did. And we served every parent tea with courtesy, and respect.'

Yasaswy attended Sukumaran's daughter's wedding. 'He noticed I'd placed directional signs at every junction,' Sukumaran laughed. 'Yasaswy said, "Didn't need a guide; your arrows were perfect."' A small line, yet one Sukumaran never forgot.

To Sukumaran, Yasaswy was a leader who could envision an Everest and calmly hand you the first rope. He was a general without a uniform who found in others the perfect soldiers for his education war.

The Phantom Brand

Magnus was the guerrilla-style squad operating without the ICFAI brand name. The ICFAI tag was not placed in the prospectus, ads, or billboards. The idea was to assess whether it could grow on its own.

This would have made sense if Yasaswy were merely a franchisee of the ICFAI brand, but he wasn't. He was its owner. So, was he responding to an intellectual challenge, or was there something deeper at play?

'Magnus was an experiment in anonymity,' someone said. It would prove that the ICFAI model wasn't brand-dependent if it could stand on its own feet. It was launched with no legacy and almost no time.

In March, Yasaswy called for a prospectus. He wanted the first campuses up by July. That gave the team three months to staff, design, market and recruit.

In a frenzy of activity, Magnus was launched in eleven cities including Hyderabad, Vizag, Bangalore, Bhubaneswar, Chennai, Coimbatore, Kochi, Pune, Kolhapur and Nagpur. Each location had rented premises, temporary signage, and plywood partitions for classrooms.

But beneath the surface, everything ran like ICFAI: common HR, shared accounts, central coordination, and academic rigour.

In sixty days, Magnus conducted two hundred and fifty events, including counselling meets, achiever talks, industry panels, and faculty demos.

Students showed up. In Hyderabad, the inaugural batch had a hundred students. Bangalore brought in eighty, Vizag sixty, and even smaller centres like Kolhapur and Coimbatore pulled twenty-five to forty each.

By the third year, Magnus showed a modest surplus.

Comparisons with INC began. Both targeted similar students. Magnus had the edge in Vizag, Bangalore, and Bhubaneswar. But INC scaled wider. With a hundred and seventy-three campuses at its peak, it became the dominant player. Magnus stayed boutique. If INC chased volume, Magnus sought validation.

By 2010, Indian regulators were tightening oversight of management education. ICFAI and its affiliate, Magnus School of Business, had to adapt or step aside. It decided not to admit a new batch in 2011. The last cohort was admitted in 2010, and arrangements were made to ensure they graduated with placements and support.

But this wasn't an exit; it was a pivot.

Yasaswy devised a new strategy: apply for AICTE approval to launch Postgraduate Diploma in Management (PGDM) programmes at four locations: Hyderabad, Nagpur, and two campuses in Raipur.

Two would run under the Magnus name (Le Magnus School of Management) and two under IBS, which here stood for 'The Institute of Business Studies'—not 'ICFAI Business School.' The idea was to operate through different societies: the Magnus Society for the Magnus-branded campuses and the ICFAI Society for the IBS ones.

In Raipur, ICFAI had two parcels of land: sixty acres for Magnus and another forty acres for ICFAI. Both campuses received AICTE approvals, first Magnus and later IBS. The process was repeated successfully in Nagpur and Hyderabad.

But just as everything was ready—ads released, faculty hired, infrastructure in place—Yasaswy called for a halt. The IBS-branded ones were paused. Only the two Magnus-branded campuses admitted students from the four approved campuses.

The exact reasons for not going ahead with the IBS campuses weren't known, but those close to him suspected he wanted to test the waters without diluting the IBS name. Yet the very act of securing approvals signalled intent—that ICFAI could play by the rulebook if it chose.

Magnus ran its programmes briefly before Yasaswy made another decisive call—merge everything under the ICFAI umbrella.

Post-merger, the fates of the four centres diverged:

- Raipur (Magnus Campus): The sixty-acre property was sold to an external buyer.
- Raipur (IBS Campus): This became ICFAI University, Raipur.
- Hyderabad (Magnus at Suchitra): This became the academic back-end office of ICFAI.
- Nagpur (IBS near Amravati Road): This remains unused but intact, with land and buildings in place.

Behind the scenes, E.N. Murthy played a big role. A former banker, he was once the controller of examinations at ICFAI and part of the innermost circle. 'Murthy wasn't loud, but his initials were on every file that mattered.' As the head of finance, legal, HR, registrations, and vigilance, Murthy was Yasaswy's go-to man for compliance and approvals.

The AICTE approval story was a first for ICFAI. Unlike its university ventures, ICFAI had now voluntarily entered the regulatory maze, proving that compliance and creativity could coexist.

Behind the launch of Magnus lies an untold story. The institution first began as a coaching centre to prepare students for IBSAT, the common admission test for IBS, as well as for CAT, the national Common Admission Test. It didn't do well. Then Yasaswy repositioned the centre with a college focus. From a tutorial to a B-School with a university degree, all in under ten years, was some stretch! It was one of those Yasaswy moves that turned failure into rehearsal.

In October 2002, Amit Bhadra, a former entrepreneur, attended an interview that would ultimately impact thousands of management students across India. The ad that brought him there had read: 'Looking for IIM graduates to lead ambitious projects.'

Across the table sat N.J. Yasaswy.

The meeting was short and unspectacular. Just one man and one round. At the end of it, Yasaswy said, 'Join our IKC.'

The ICFAI Knowledge Centre (IKC) was an innovation hub. It was filled with IIT and IIM alumni, and it ran on caffeine, conviction, and ideas. You could propose a project, and if Yasaswy saw potential, he would greenlight it.

The first time they met, Yasaswy walked over to a counter in his office, picked a tea sachet, brewed it himself, and handed it to Bhadra. It was a small gesture, but it signalled the kind of leadership he practised—quiet, gracious, and deeply intentional. That cup of tea would become Bhadra's first lesson in humility with authority.

A few months later, in early 2003, Yasaswy called Bhadra for another conversation. 'Magnus Institute,' he said. 'It's bleeding. But it has potential. Would you like to take it over?'

Magnus, as we know, was ICFAI's play in the MBA test-prep space—twenty-seven centres across nineteen cities, well-staffed, well-equipped, and woefully underperforming. Losses were piling up, and the morale was low. Most leaders would have shut it down. Yasaswy didn't.

He didn't see a broken model. He saw a fractured narrative. And he needed someone who could re-script it.

He chose Bhadra, maybe because he had worked across geographies. To support him, Sudhakar Rao,* a young IIM Bangalore graduate, was assigned. Together, they met Ranga Rao, then head of Magnus. Within days, the baton was formally passed.

Bhadra became the head of Magnus, with Sudhakar Rao as Associate Head.

Then came May 2003.

Chhattisgarh had just passed a Private Universities Act. Yasaswy said, 'We'll establish two universities—one under ICFAI and another under a new brand: Le Magnus University,' he said. The coaching centres would morph into something larger: the Magnus School of Business (MSB). They now offered a full-fledged MBA.

'You have forty-five days,' he added. 'Curriculum, faculty, infrastructure, admissions. Build it.'

There was one catch: ICFAI's name would not appear. The university had to stand on its own credibility.

Bhadra and Sudhakar hit the ground running. They toured twenty cities, built an academic core in Hyderabad, recruited leadership with IIT and IIM backgrounds, and leaned into one defining proposition: quality education at an accessible price. With minimal budget, they resorted to just phone calls,

---

*Sudhakar Rao is one of the authors of this book, *The Man Who Saw Tomorrow*.

outreach, and an iron-clad belief in what they were building.

They were running a start-up disguised as a university project.

The first batch had three hundred and forty-two students. The next, four hundred and forty-five. Then nine hundred and fifty. Then one thousand two hundred and fifty. By 2007, MSB had crossed three thousand students annually.

Throughout, Yasaswy remained laser-focused on one thing: academic integrity. 'He never asked about revenue,' Bhadra later said. 'He wanted to know: Are they learning? Are we improving?'

There were no donation seats.

Bhadra was given sweeping autonomy—he could hire, promote, rent campuses, and sanction budgets. It was trust without interference, supervision without suffocation. He created a high-trust environment where results mattered, but methods mattered more.

He even found time to conduct sessions on 'Creating Magic in the Classroom'. His case study, a global fashion brand sourcing yarn from Egypt, buttons from China, stitching from Hong Kong, design from France advertising from the US, and sales all over North America and Western Europe, became a mini masterclass on international business. To young faculty, it felt like attending a Harvard lecture in a Hyderabad conference room.

In 2007, Bhadra and Rao travelled with Yasaswy to the AACSB (Association to Advance Collegiate Schools of Business, the world's leading accreditation authority) Conference in Florida, and visited top US business schools. The learnings from that trip—around faculty sabbaticals, global accreditations and academic branding—found their way back into MSB. It was one of the few times Bhadra had seen Yasaswy take notes. He even talked of building overseas campuses one day, quietly sketching futures others couldn't yet see.

As India's regulatory frameworks evolved, so did ICFAI's institutional strategy. Several states had passed Private Universities Acts. ICFAI chose to focus on building multi-discipline universities within those states rather than expanding stand-alone schools nationwide.

By early 2009, Bhadra stepped away from Magnus. He had other commitments. It felt like the right time to hand over the reins. He continued to be in touch with Yasaswy and other colleagues at ICFAI.

The Magnus experiment was undertaken to assess the potential for scaling up across geographies with a new brand. In 2010, ICFAI successfully established universities in several states that had enacted the Private Universities Act. Magnus was not there in any of these states. ICFAI had decided to focus on the university model for scaling up as opposed to running stand-alone schools. The exceptions were the first-generation IBS. The Magnus experiment had thus run its course. Admissions to the Magnus School of Business were discontinued in 2011, and the school closed after the enrolled students graduated.

But its lessons remained. Magnus had proven that anonymity could teach.

Years later, someone asked Amit Bhadra to rank the best leaders he'd worked with—Harvard DBAs, billionaires, corporate giants. He smiled and said comparisons were unfair, but remarked, 'N.J. Yasaswy was one of the finest leaders and among the most brilliant this country has produced. Not just in education. Anywhere.'

The Fire Engine

That year, the Supreme Court struck down the recognition of hundred and four private universities in Chhattisgarh. Magnus was one of them. The ruling wasn't directed at Magnus, but the panic and anger were.

Act I: Chennai

Usually placid Chennai was livid. A manager had mishandled things, and students threatened violence.

Headquarters wanted to send a senior officer to defuse it.

'No,' Rao said. 'They need someone they trust.'

Yasaswy hesitated. 'You don't have to go.'

'Sir, my bag's already packed.'

At the gate, a police escort joined his car. The students shouted, 'He's brought the police!'

Rao replied, 'The inspector will wait outside. Let's talk.'

Inside, he asked, 'Where's your list of demands?'

'They're…not typed yet.'

He walked to a computer. 'Dictate. I'll type.'

He corrected their grammar, strengthened two points, signed, and said, 'Now go study. Exams are coming.'

Back in Hyderabad, someone whispered, 'You signed it? Without legal clearance?'

Yasaswy's reply was simple: 'We'll stand by it.'

Later, he caught Rao's eye and nodded. It was silent approval—the kind that meant everything.

Magnus limped on, issuing certificates through partner universities until its final closure.

It may have faded from public memory, but for those who lived it, the Fire Engine moment proved one thing: leadership is not about avoiding crises, but absorbing them with grace.

When Sudhakar Rao and his team met Yasaswy that morning with a copy of the judgement, Yasaswy said quietly: 'Meet the students. Meet the parents. Explain to them. Don't argue. Stay calm. Show them the facts. And no debates, please.'

It sounded simple but it was a fire-drill for leadership under flame. There were eleven campuses, eleven bonfires of rage.

Act II: Hyderabad

At the Himayat Nagar campus, tension hung heavy. Students paced the corridors, angry and uncertain.

The Centre Head let the audience vent it out until the shouting turned into silence. Only then did he begin.

Once that was over, Sudhakar asked, 'How many of you haven't been placed?'

Silence.

He pointed one by one. 'HSBC?' 'HDFC?' He knew the list. He had it memorized. 'You are placed, so what's your problem?'

A boy muttered. 'I am placed, but not everyone is.'

'Then speak for yourself.'

You don't argue with a mob. You outlast it. By evening, the air had cooled. When Yasaswy, hear, he smiled and told Sudhakar, 'I intuitively knew you'd handle it.'

The kind of quiet approval meant more than a hundred standing ovations.

Act III: Bhubaneswar

Here the protests were louder.

Rao spent the day talking, listening and absorbing. At night, as dinner arrived at his hotel, the receptionist called: 'Sir...the students are here. They say you're not leaving.'

'Let them in.'

Ten boys stormed in. Sudhakar told them, 'In ten minutes, the police will be here.'

'Why?'

'This is a hotel. If ten angry boys land up in a room, the front desk doesn't need a memo to act.'

Right on cue, the bell rang.

'Everything okay, Sir?' the cop asked.

Rao greeted the officer with a smile. 'Everything's fine. These are my friends.'

One by one, the boys left. Some fires, Rao realized, die when met with calm air.

A College Called Meritum

They thought he was dreaming out loud the first time he described it.

'We'll build a college,' Yasaswy said. 'Not like the ones India already has. This one will make thinkers. With ethics in their spine, logic in their minds, and fire in their belly.'

Yasaswy wasn't interested in churning out commerce graduates who could recite ratios. He wanted graduates who could think, speak, argue, and he wasn't waiting for India to be ready. He was building what it needed.

The name came first. *Meritum*—Latin for 'merit'. The year was 2001. That year, the BBA (Honours) programme was launched. Each batch had just thirty students—by design. The faculty were mentors, not graders.

One Monday morning, in a class on ethics, a student interrupted. 'Why are we reading Plato?'

The professor didn't flinch. 'Because you'll one day write a business code. Better you read someone who helped write a republic.'

This wasn't a place for soft landings. The trimester system was packed with logic, history, ethics, economics, communication, and reading lists. Students read Rabindranath Tagore and Thomas Paine not because it was trendy but because it was necessary.

Meritum graduates walked out with minds sharpened.

They could think on their feet, speak without hesitating, and defend an idea without collapsing into clichés.

In a country obsessed with placements, Meritum quietly trained citizens. Some now lead fintech teams, others teach at community colleges, and a few draft policy briefs for institutions they once had to Google.

Even the best ideas sometimes arrive too soon. Meritum wasn't a recognized university. It hit the same hurdles, raised questions, and met the same fate as the other early experiments. Eventually, it wound down. The students graduated, the teachers moved on, and the hostel lights flickered out.

Yasaswy, watching quietly, said, 'Maybe we were ten years too early. But someone had to try.' Then he turned the page. 'One day, India will have colleges like this. Ones that blend discipline with dialogue, knowledge with wisdom, competition with compassion.' And maybe he was right. Ashoka. Krea. FLAME. All came a decade later. They built on a dream that had been dared before.

He built INC for access, Magnus for audacity, and Meritum for ideals. Together they formed a trilogy of intent—three experiments in scale, stealth and soul. INC reached out to the towns India forgot. Magnus tested whether ideas could walk without a name. Meritum asked what would happen if education rediscovered its conscience.

Chapter 11

He Walked with Them

By the early 1990s, as ICFAI found its legs, Yasaswy began shaping not just an institution but a generation of thinkers.

Some arrived from IIM. Others came from banks, the army, boardrooms and bus stops. He didn't care for pedigree; he cared for spark. And when he found it, he'd hand you a map and throw you straight into the deep end with a smile and no life jacket.

This is the story of the ones who didn't drown, and learned to swim. These were not employees. They were his fire starters, men he ignited and trusted to carry the flame.

T. Krishna Mohan traded a stable job at TI Diamond Chain for a seat in front of a fire, more precisely, in front of N.J. Yasaswy, his father's cousin.

'My son,' his dad had said, 'if you want to learn, follow him. But brace yourself.'

'Yasaswy never eased you in,' Krishna recalls. 'He threw you straight into the deep end and expected you to swim—fast.' Those who worked with him learned one thing quickly; the day started fast and only got faster.

Yasaswy didn't wait for approval, data, or even content to be ready. His philosophy was simple: release first and perfect later. But the gap between the two steps was in days, not weeks.

When he decided to launch a course in technical analysis, he didn't set up a panel of experts. He drafted a newspaper ad that morning, booked the space by noon, and assembled the team that night. He was that fast.

'Do today's work today; and tomorrow's, too, if possible.' That was his motto. Krishna had to adjust fast.

Krishna began as a research assistant at YMA, helping Yasaswy publish *IMA*, the weekly stock market newsletter. Later, he became his executive assistant, managing his schedule.

Then came the next nudge: 'Do CFA.' Krishna says, 'I followed his lead, and once I qualified, he asked me to coordinate ICFAI's MDP.' And one day he posed a new challenge: 'Why don't you present a few topics yourself?'

'Me? But I've never spoken in public.'

'Then it's time you start. I'll help you prepare.'

And he did—reviewing slides, sharpening arguments, trimming jokes, and adding punch lines.

He first let Krishna sit through a few of his sessions and then sat through Krishna's early talks, and offered tips on engaging an audience. One talk became two. Two became ten. 'After that, I was on the speaker's list for all ICFAI seminars.'

Krishna soon earned more than just proximity. He earned trust.

'We wanted to demystify finance,' Krishna says. 'This was before financial literacy became a buzzword. Back then, mutual funds were a mystery to most. Our job was to make investing feel possible.'

Krishna had to draft, revise, lay out the text, cross-check sources, and ensure every comma was correct.

'There was no email back then. Instructions came via phone or from across the desk. And if you said something was eighty per cent done, bring the eighty per cent, he would say.'

That line became infamous in the office because often

the eighty per cent didn't exist. It was a bluff, and Yasaswy knew how to call it.

'He wasn't unreasonable, but he was demanding. If the work fell short, he made sure everyone knew. Voices could rise.

'The first two months were intense. He expected quality but he calmed down once he saw that I delivered. Then, strangely enough, he started telling me, "You don't have to be so perfect. Ninety-five per cent is fine."'

That was classic Yasaswy—harsh until he saw commitment, then gentle. He respected competence. Once convinced, he defended you even against himself. Slowly, he inducted Krishna Mohan as his executive assistant. Krishna became a gatekeeper.

'People would ask me, "How is Sir's mood today?"' Krishna laughs. 'If I said the *tandoor* (clay oven) was *garam* (hot), they'd turn around.'

There were also moments of contradiction.

One morning, Yasaswy was due to deliver a keynote lecture. He had asked a faculty member to help him with the material. However, he received no update until the morning of the talk.

'Where is he?' Yasaswy asked.

'He hasn't come in,' Krishna reported.

'Go get him.'

Krishna drove across town to the man's house. The man was visibly ill and running a fever. Krishna suggested he stay home, but the man insisted, buttoned up, and got in the car.

As they entered the office, Yasaswy stood up. One look, and he snapped. 'What nonsense is this? Why did you bring him here?'

'He wanted to come,' Krishna stammered.

Yasaswy turned to the man. 'Go home. You're not well. I'm sorry, but you need to rest.'

The contradiction stayed with Krishna. 'He was furious. But even in anger, there was fairness.'

That complexity was Yasaswy's signature. He could scorch and soothe in the same breath. He wasn't interested in appearances. Even in public seminars, when asked how long the CFA programme would last, he didn't bluff. 'If it doesn't last, it doesn't,' he'd say. 'Nothing lasts forever.'

Krishna helped him write books on investments.

'He'd give me chapter titles,' Krishna recalls. 'I'd gather material, format it. Then we'd revise, iterate, and send to Vision Books.'

'Even small things like which quote to open with or which graph to cut, would be discussed.'

If the first ten years of N.J. Yasaswy's professional life were a blaze of brilliance, the next ten were filled with bruises, bankrupt dreams, and battles lost.

He once told Krishna Mohan, 'I lost ten years of my life. Between my late twenties and late thirties. Wasted.' He was referring to the manufacturing meltdown.

Years later, Krishna would reflect on why so many people stayed loyal. 'It wasn't just vision,' he says. 'It was velocity.'

When you worked with him, your days moved fast. Your thoughts sharpened. Your standards changed. You became allergic to mediocrity.

By 1997, Krishna had worn every hat: writer, editor, assistant. Each one fit tighter than the last. He wanted to explore more. So, when the opportunity to go to the US came, he checked with Yasaswy. The Big Man said he must take it for the experience that international exposure brings.

Today, Krishna Mohan is a freelancing software architect in the US after being a Principal Member of ERP Systems at Verizon.

But to this day, every time he finishes a task early, he hears that old voice in his head: 'Good. Now start tomorrow's.'

Stone That Smelled of Jasmine

'Joy,' Yasaswy said, 'you've been a banker. Can you build an institution?'

Joy had built loan books, risk models, and branch teams. But an institution? 'I'll try,' he said.

Yasaswy slid a file across the table like a chess move. 'Start here.'

That was 1994. From that moment, Joy's world exploded. Joy's life began to accelerate, and never quite slowed again.

The interview should've ended there. But Yasaswy wasn't done. 'Life here is like being inside a pressure cooker. Don't say I didn't warn you.'

Joy, a thirty-something officer from Federal Bank who had just cleared his CFA after six years of late nights, didn't think twice. 'I'm already in one, Sir. This can't be worse.'

He had no idea there were pressure cookers and then there was ICFAI.

When Joy arrived in Hyderabad that August, he expected a formal orientation. What he got instead was silence. For two weeks, he tried without luck to meet Yasaswy.

Finally, someone passed on the message: 'Let him look around, meet people and get to know things. There's no hurry to see me.'

So, Joy listened, watched, and asked questions. After two weeks, he met Yasaswy. The conversations would stretch across years, punctuated by nudges and provocation.

'Never use force when persuasion can work,' Yasaswy told him after a bruising meeting. 'If someone resists, don't push. Turn the idea until it becomes theirs.'

Yasaswy did not have artworks in his room. Instead, he had stacks of brochures from Harvard, Stanford, and Wharton—all ordered by post. He used them to learn how an Indian underdog could match the Ivy League standards.

'Knowledge,' he told Joy, 'is the cheapest form of power. You just have to ask.'

Joy came from operations, having spent fourteen years in banking. He didn't know marketing from mango-pickle, but Yasaswy didn't care. He threw him into sales promotion. His first assignment: market ICFAI's Transworld MBA in the Middle East.

Joy had never stepped outside India. Nervously, he asked if Yasaswy had any contacts in Dubai.

'Of course,' Yasaswy said. 'But most of them are in jail.'

It wasn't literal, The message meant: 'Don't lean on me. Find your own ground.'

At ICFAI, marketing was elegant warfare. The FDP was one such weapon—training thousands of faculties across disciplines free of cost—including travel, food and accommodation. Joy helped scale it. They weren't merely workshops, but mini Trojan horses of goodwill, meant to sow respect and repayable later with cold calls.

At ICFAI, some of Joy's ideas were shot down. When he proposed opening regional centres in four metros, the Board frowned. 'Why spend when email exists?' This even though Yasaswy had already approved it privately.

Yasaswy stayed quiet during the meeting. Later, he called Joy. 'Rewrite it. Tone it down. Try again.'

It passed the second time around. That was typical Yasaswy: he'd let you stumble once, so you'd learn how to rise on your own.

Of course, there were darker days. One Sunday brought scandal: someone had leaked the CFA exam papers. The credibility of the entire programme teetered. Within hours, Yasaswy, Joy, and E.N. Murthy, were seated in the boardroom.

'Who's responsible?' Yasaswy asked. His voice was calm but cold.

They traced the leak. The next three hours were spent on damage control: legal calls, press drafts, and exam restructuring.

Yasaswy was clear that they must be transparent about what happened. 'No institution fails because it makes a mistake,' he said. 'It fails when it hides it.'

By evening, there was a plan. By midnight, an email. And by morning, a crisis contained.

In 2001, Joy decided to leave. Reliance's offer to help set up a university was too tempting to refuse. Joy could not bring himself to tell the man who had turned him from a banker into an education evangelist.

That morning, he opened his Bible. His eyes fell on Ecclesiastes:

Ecclesiastes 3:1–8

1 There is a time for everything,
and a season for every activity under the heavens:
2 a time to be born and a time to die,
a time to plant and a time to uproot

It felt like the verse had been waiting for him. He framed it, as much to remind himself as to explain his decision.

When he broke the news, Yasaswy tried to buy time. 'Take a vacation,' he said. 'Go to Kerala. Think it over.'

Joy had already thought it through. Even Yasaswy, the man he revered the most, next only to his father, couldn't convince him. When Joy gifted him the frame, Yasaswy read it and smiled faintly, and without a word kept it on his desk.

Joy continued to contact Yasaswy, visiting him whenever he came to Hyderabad. The frame sat on Yasaswy's desk for years, along with photographs of his father and Abraham Lincoln.

In Malayalam, there's a saying: *Mulla poompodi ettu kidakkum kallinumundoru sourabhyam* —the stone that treads on jasmine carries its fragrance. Yasaswy was the jasmine. And those who walked with him carried that fragrance forever.

The Philosopher's Echo

At Tata Steel's Vizag outpost, where he worked, everything in the life of the IIT-IIM alumnus A.V. Vedpuriswar looked good.

Except that his mind was beginning to rust. He wanted to move out of operations into something that challenged his mind. So, late one night, he wrote to an address in Hyderabad: ICFAI.

The very next day, the phone rang. 'This is Yasaswy.'

Within a week, Ved was on a train to Hyderabad to meet the silver-haired visionary who sold ideas faster than you could say 'hello'.

Yasaswy spoke of a self-funded university with Indian roots but global reach, of case studies written by Indian hands, and how these will one day upstage the global leaders. The offer was generous and Ved didn't think twice. The year was 1996.

Thirty years and three jobs later, Ved remembers working on multiple things and seeing his boss work from close quarters.

'One week, I would build finance content, and the next moment, I would organize a national seminar.' No two days were alike. Each day felt like a new course—designed, delivered, and graded overnight.

Before Ved's first session at IBS, Yasaswy scanned his notes, and said, 'Don't lecture. Ask questions.'

Then, in the margins, he scribbled: 'Why did the RBI cut interest rates that year?' 'Why did IBM exit the PC business?'

'They've read the headlines,' he said. 'Make them read between the lines.'

By the mid-nineties, Yasaswy pushed for a Harvard

collaboration on case studies. When the cases arrived, he ran sessions himself and told the faculty to 'Master the theory' but not to let it 'straitjacket the debate'.

He didn't just want to import excellence. So, he set up the Case Development Cell and manned it with young talent. Most had never written a case before, but that didn't matter. Ved was asked to lead it.

In time, those cases travelled—first across India, then to classrooms half a world away.

By 2005, Ved moved on, his personality rewired by Yasaswy, his thinking sharper, and his curiosity restless.

The Professor from Godrej

Naveen Das didn't start out in academics.

He joined the Godrej Group as an engineer from IIT Kharagpur with a management degree from IIM Calcutta. It was a stable and respected career, but over time it lost its spark.

He felt the need for change and contacted his IIM senior, A.V. Vedpuriswar.

Ved didn't hesitate. 'Come try ICFAI,' he said.

Naveen flew to Hyderabad and joined as a faculty member on 1 September 1999. His practical, jargon-free, industry-rooted teaching clicked with students, and word spread quickly.

That's when N.J. Yasaswy stepped in with a challenge. Ved had begun writing global cases. He was writing about global companies like McDonald's or Nordstrom, but hardly any about Indian companies like Bharti and Dr. Reddy's.

'Let's build Indian cases,' Yasaswy told Naveen. And with that single line, the ICFAI Center for Management Research (ICMR) was born, with Naveen at the helm.

At its peak, ICMR had over forty researchers churning out Indian case studies, simple textbooks, and curated reading material. *The Economist Style Guide* became their Bible. Every sentence had to be clear, concise, and readable to a reasonably educated Indian.

The model proved successful and was later replicated at ICFAI campuses in Bangalore, Ahmedabad, and Pune.

But the real learning was the review meetings with Yasaswy. 'He'd walk in and take complete charge,' Naveen recalls. 'He remembered every detail—what had been promised, what was pending.'

You couldn't hide behind PowerPoints or polite phrases. If something was delayed or missing, he would ask directly.

But these meetings weren't just audits; they were masterclasses. Yasaswy often ended them by handing out articles, book clippings, or case studies.

'We came out feeling like we'd just heard a TED Talk.'

Then came a personal loss. In 2004, Naveen suddenly lost his father. Yasaswy arranged tickets before Naveen could ask and deputed Ved to go along with him. It was leadership without announcement.

Naveen was transferred to Kolkata. From there, he replicated the ICMR model across eastern India. In 2010, he decided to move on. It had been a transformative journey.

There Were Others

In 1993, the year Tendulkar bowled that heroic last over in the Hero Cup to outsmart South Africa, an unlikely debut was unfolding on a different pitch. S. Sridhar, hungry for a shot at journalism, dropped in uninvited at 52 Nagarjuna Hills. In another world, he might've been turned away at the gate. But at ICFAI, he found himself face to face with N.J. Yasaswy.

Most bosses would've waved him off, but Yasaswy didn't. Without a single formal question, he offered Sridhar a job with a salary of ₹2,500 a month. That was a jackpot, but the real windfall came later.

'Nobody taught me how to think like he did,' Sridhar recalls. 'He'd nudge me to look at Alvin Toffler, Peter Drucker, Charles Handy, Edward de Bono and the like. "Read them," he'd say. "Then come tell me if you agree."'

And Sridhar began thinking sharper, reading deeper, and writing bolder. 'He mentored by magnetism,' says Sridhar, now a Family Office Consultant who in between spent several years in the banking industry.

And Sridhar wasn't alone.

When R.S. Prasad joined ICFAI to handle media relations, he wasn't handed a manual. Instead, he got a mantra. 'Never say the media is critical of us. It's our job to enlighten them.'

So, Prasad met one journalist every fortnight, and what he saw changed his idea of leadership. If a journalist asked for time, Yasaswy would cancel meetings, shift appointments, and offer his unhurried attention.

He welcomed even those who had criticized ICFAI. 'Invite them too,' he'd say. 'Especially them.'

'I saw journalists walk out of his office visibly moved,' Prasad recalls. 'He didn't defend education. He made them care about it.'

Yasaswy's mentoring was never about lofty lectures. It showed up in quiet gestures like the kind V.R. Sankara remembers vividly. Sankara first met Yasaswy in a bookstore. 'He looked like he belonged equally in a finance seminar and a film set,' says Sankara.

They worked together at HIFCO and *Current Investments India*, YMA's investment magazine.

It was early days, and Sankara was still testing his wings. One evening in Vijayawada, after successfully organizing an investor meeting, the two were scheduled to return to

Hyderabad by train. But Yasaswy quietly cancelled the ticket.

'We're flying,' he said. It was Sankara's first-ever flight.

'It was his way of showing appreciation,' says the man who now runs the ICFAI Society.

What made Yasaswy's mentorship different was that it never came with a manual or a halo.

He didn't hand you a ladder. He gave you a map and trusted you to walk. He didn't reward talent with comfort. He rewarded it with challenge. And above all, he mentored people to help them become more of who they already were.

The Difficult Boss

In the summer of 1998, forty-three-year-old K. Seethapathi made a defining decision. His bank transferred him to Mumbai, but since his children's schooling was a priority, he stayed on in Hyderabad. He was walking towards an uncertainty that would later define him.

He reached out to Associate Dean T. Ravikumar, an old acquaintance. Within days, a meeting with N.J. Yasaswy was fixed. Initially, the tone was warm, as both men were from Guntur, alumni of the same school, with Seethapathi being a few years junior. They shared camaraderie over common friends and childhood memories. Then, Yasaswy shifted gears.

'You're leaving a stable banking career. That's not a casual step,' he said. 'We can match your salary. But this isn't just a job change; it's a sea change in orbit. You must speak to your family.'

Seethapathi joined ICFAI's academic wing as a faculty member. It was a compact unit of twenty people tasked with writing and updating self-learning materials. Under Yasaswy's relentless scrutiny, every page had to be robust, relevant and industry-aligned.

When ICFAI launched its programme in Treasury and Forex Management (TFM), Seethapathi's expertise came in useful. He built a simulated dealing room, with software and mock trades, thus pioneering market-ready education.

Curriculum design was always in-house. Yasaswy handpicked subject matter experts. Then Seethapathi's team would debate and draft. Yasaswy was a man of detail who knew 'what skills the market hadn't asked for yet, but soon would.'

The two developed mutual respect.

But one evening, things came to a head. A high-voltage disagreement erupted over a matter that shall stay private, and Yasaswy's words stung.

After the meeting, Seethapathi walked straight to E.N. Murthy. 'This is not what I signed up for,' he said. 'I can go back to Bombay. My forex credentials are still bankable. '

The next morning, Murthy told Seethapathi: 'The boss wants to see you.'

What followed wasn't an apology; it was an anchor. For ninety minutes, Yasaswy listened, clarified, and then said, 'If your elder brother scolds you, does that mean he doesn't care? You matter here. And I will never go easy on people I value.'

From that day, things changed. The work didn't get easier, but the trust grew stronger. Soon, Seethapathi was asked to join faculty recruitment at INC. Over four years, along with R. Prasad (whom we shall soon meet), he hired three thousand faculty members across hundred and fifty campuses, interviewing more than ten thousand candidates.

High-stakes assignments followed, including resolving law programme protests, designing frameworks for Alpha Foundation and CP Brown Academy, and mentoring young faculty.

In 2007, Yasaswy asked, 'Why haven't you finished your PhD?'

Seethapathi explained that given his myriad responsibilities, there wasn't sufficient time. Yasaswy wasn't moved.

'You're leading PhDs without being one. You're capable.' Then, with a tone both stern and kind, he moved him to a lighter role. 'Finish it. Return stronger. And I will give you back your present job.'

Soon came an offer from a private player at double the pay. When the mentee spoke to his mentor, Yasaswy asked Seethapathi to stay. But the offer was too good to pass up. Yasaswy agreed, saying, 'For you, the door is always open.'

In 2013, Seeethapathi walked back through that door. Years later, he'd say, 'Yasaswy believed in me long before I believed in myself.'

❧

In a world where mentors come with titles, Yasaswy was a gardener. He spotted a seed, watered it, and waited for it to sprout. He never insisted it become a certain kind of tree.

Perhaps that's the highest form of mentorship. He didn't just build ICFAI; he built the people who would one day build futures of their own.

PART IV

Republic of Learning

An investment in knowledge pays the best interest.

—BENJAMIN FRANKLIN

Chapter 12

Learing Without Walls

Nelson Mandela called education the most powerful weapon to change the world. Yasaswy agreed, but added a clause: the weapon be delivered, not merely designed. In his view, the classroom didn't need four walls. It needed relevance. If a student couldn't come to the learning, then learning had to pack its bags and travel to the student.

It was 1985—and it was an India between two worlds, viz., rotary phones and rising ambition. Rajiv Gandhi was Prime Minister. The Berlin Wall still stood. Shah Rukh Khan, Salman Khan and Aamir Khan were just names in a phonebook. Sachin Tendulkar hadn't played a single professional game. And Dhirubhai Ambani was the pied piper of Dalal Street.

In Hyderabad, N.J. Yasaswy had bet on the high-stakes CFA programme—a course that would be taught without a campus, delivered without boundaries.

Back then, correspondence education was seen as the last resort of the underprepared. Yasaswy saw it not as a shortcut but as a long bridge. Not a distant cousin of classroom instruction but a close confidant, as a long bridge.

'Distance,' he insisted, 'should never be a disqualifier.' And with a half-smile, he added, 'Mark it, one day people will sit in their pyjamas and earn degrees.'

The press laughed. He didn't. Two decades later, the world would stop laughing.

CFA was the seed, not the tree. He didn't know its final shape, only that it would grow. He often said that there was no grand strategy behind the success. It was just a series of small steps that turned out to be right. But one thing was clear in his mind. He wasn't chasing a product; he was designing a possibility. He wanted to reimagine education.

While most educationalists tried to catch them young, Yasaswy turned towards corporate India. That first batch had seventeen and in it was an army colonel trading war stories for case studies, a stockbroker debating derivatives, and a teacher solving financial simulations.

In later years, many of those students came back, not just to say thank you but to contribute. They became part of the faculty, the councils, and the inner circle. Yasaswy didn't just want learners. He wanted builders.

One afternoon in the early 2000s, a handful of senior team members sat, eyes fixed on the man by the window.

Yasaswy stood with arms folded, watching the clouds roll over the Hyderabad skyline. 'Distance learning,' he said quietly, 'isn't a side project. It's the main road for most of India. For those who can't come here but still want to go far.'

He wasn't worried about repeating himself. He had said something similar twenty years earlier, which still held true.

'Campus programmes select who gets in. But distance learning?' He paused. 'It reveals who has the grit to finish.'

A younger colleague leaned in. 'So, Sir, entry doesn't matter?'

'I'm saying exit matters more,' he replied. 'We don't reward attendance. We reward endurance.'

Whenever someone proposed diluting exams or trimming content, someone else would quote him: 'We reward those who finish.'

It was still early days for edtech. 'We're not chasing technology,' he told his product head once. 'We're using it to chase the learner.'

The team walked in with charts and theories when online MBA enrolments began to slide.

'Engagement is low,' one said.

'Too much competition,' said another.

Yasaswy heard them all out. Then, in his usual unhurried tone, he said, 'Let's build a cafeteria, not a mess hall. Let students pick what they want, when they want. It's their plate.'

And the pivot began.

'You don't drop out of a distance learning programme because you're lazy,' he said. 'You drop out because life doesn't pause for your syllabus. So we have to design for that.'

The material became more grounded. Case studies were drawn from Indian markets, and professors started thinking more like product designers.

Not everything worked. Some programmes never took off. Others fizzled out after a few batches.

But the idea endured.

Students logged in after night shifts in Bhubaneswar. Homemakers watched finance lectures in the quiet after their children had gone to bed. Soldiers in remote bases downloaded modules on patchy connections. These were the people he built for, not the privileged, but the persistent.

A hand went up. 'But regulations are tightening. Isn't this risky?'

He turned slowly. 'What's riskier?' he asked. 'Betting on the future or clinging to the past?' That was his style. He would reframe the question until your own logic betrayed your fear.

Because distance learning was never about pyjamas or bandwidth. It was about giving people the tools to finish what they started.

And that was the future Yasaswy always bet on.

But we have got far ahead of the story. Let's return to how distance learning, once the cash cow, was built and scaled up.

He Sold Learning

It all began with a VHS tape whirring inside a VCR.

The tape had arrived in a plain brown envelope, along with a neatly printed prospectus and an invitation to Sanjay Ramchandani to attend a post-budget lecture. The tape was an ICFAI advertorial and stood out because it was a form educational institutions don't do.

Sanjay attended the lecture and was moved. 'He wasn't flashy,' Sanjay recalled later. 'But the way he linked the budget to the stock market—I hadn't heard anyone speak like that.'

The hook landed. Sanjay signed up for the CFA course. In 1996, he arrived in Hyderabad for his CFA convocation. A casual post-conversation chat turned into an impromptu interview with Ravi Kumar, then Dean of Academics, and ICFAI senior E.N. Murthy.

'You did CFA?' Yasaswy asked.

'Yes, Sir.'

'You know the material and the promise. Would you like to sell that promise?'

'I'll surely try.'

In March 1998, Sanjay walked into ICFAI's Distance Learning Centre (DLC), unaware that he would help build a juggernaut that would one day generate ₹330 crore.

At the time, DLC consisted of only thirty people. One chaotic room handled marketing, servicing and administration. V.P. Joy headed the unit. Sanjay got a taste of it—brochure dispatch, courier follow-ups, student support, and procurement.

Along with him were Khader, Y.V.N. Srinivas and B. Srinivas Raj.

Within a year, the structure was changed. 'If our programmes are good, let us speak up, show up, and stand tall,' Yasaswy announced.

So, the department bifurcated. Servicing was assigned to E.N. Murthy, and marketing, still under Joy, was renamed the Promotion and Development Department. 'Marketing' sounded too in your face!

Sanjay began criss-crossing India by train and bus, explaining a course built for ambition. From May to September, he lived out of a suitcase. Mumbai to Chandigarh, Kolkata to Lucknow. Each stop meant pioneering ICFAI's first real push into the Hindi belt.

'Mumbai welcomed us warmly. Delhi was sceptical,' he chuckled. 'In the North, colleges saw us as private players out to sell something. In the West, we were seen as guides offering career clarity.'

Sanjay understood early that education marketing was anthropology. You had to understand people, their context, and their aspirations—not just push ads. You had to be part-researcher, part-sociologist, part-storyteller.

Wherever he went, he noticed one thing: students were curious, but had limited access to resources. That's when the idea of setting up local information centres came. They started small—Khalsa College in Mumbai got the first desk. It worked. Revenues spiked.

Encouraged, Yasaswy approved five more: Indore, Patna, Lucknow, Vadodara and Chandigarh. Joy and Sanjay travelled, furnished offices, and helped recruit the first batch of city heads.

'I didn't know I was building a network,' Sanjay smiled. 'I just wanted people to find us.'

Yasaswy would occasionally call from Hyderabad. 'How's Patna doing? Send me a photo of the first banner.' His curiosity travelled faster than the courier.

Throughout this expansion, Yasaswy asked questions. How fast could they scale? Could the quality be sustained? Was the message consistent? He wasn't micromanaging; he was measuring conviction.

The inflexion point occurred in early 2000 when Joy moved on, and Sanjay was promoted as head of marketing.

At their first review, Yasaswy posed a challenge: 'How do we push the CFA accelerated option? It's ₹18,000 upfront. Can we sell that?'

Sanjay nodded. 'Yes, Sir. If you give us more feet on the street, and better locations.'

Yasaswy agreed. Connaught Place in Delhi and Dalamal Tower at Nariman Point were chosen. Though expensive, they were at the heart of corporate India with access to working executives.

The gamble paid off.

By year end, ICFAI's marketing team had grown tenfold. Branches multiplied—first 18, then 26, then 50. Teams swelled from thirty to a thousand. Revenues leapt from ₹7.5 crore to ₹18 crore, and later vaulted past ₹100 crore.

Yasaswy didn't clap. He simply said, 'Good. Now do it again.'

They did. Multiple branches in cities became the new normal. Mumbai had seventeen. Delhi had twelve, Bangalore nine, and so on.

Their reach extended to railway stations and food courts in tech parks. Teams set up information desks at Churchgate Railway Station because that was where the crowd was and swiped credit cards in BPO canteens late night to catch the night-shift employees.

'We didn't wait for students to find us,' Sanjay said. 'We went to them.'

That outreach built a brand. Competitors copied the brochures, but nobody could match the discipline. Before long, the top line read ₹330 crore.

Instalment-based fee models boosted admissions but they also led to default rates. Students signed up and then dropped out. Word spread through online chats: 'Too tough. Avoid.'

Success, as always, came with its echo.

By 2009, the global financial crisis swept the interconnected world. It spooked corporate employees, and the tide turned. The US court ruling on CFA followed and it wasn't in ICFAI's favour. Then the Chennai judgement came. It shook ICFAI's and the community's confidence. From a high of ₹330 crore, revenue slid by half to ₹170 crore.

Yasaswy called for a return to fundamentals. 'If trust dips,' he said, 'visibility alone won't save you. You have to earn it again.'

'We withdrew from weaker markets. We cut branches. But the brand stayed strong,' Sanjay said. 'We had to revisit the basics.'

Rebuilding was complex. The brand had grown too fast. Yasaswy focused on correction. 'You cannot shout a ship into course. You steer it.' By 2011, the signs of revival began to show. But for Sanjay, the journey was complete.

'I gave it fourteen years. I never got to work in core finance,' he laughed. 'But we built something different—perhaps the first structured marketing team for higher education in India.' Then he paused. 'He taught me the arithmetic of belief—how to carry an idea to ₹300-plus crore and beyond.'

Sanjay left in 2012. Of Yasaswy, he said, 'The man gave us room to imagine. That's rare. That's why ICFAI scaled.'

But numbers were only half the story. Behind the explosive

growth lay a quiet revolution, in systems, training calendars, incentive models, and machines that did the talking.

The Bellwether of Education

The student never walked into the classroom. She stayed where she was. And Yasaswy insisted that learning had to walk into her life, not as charity, but as dignity. That was the soul of ICFAI's distance education movement—a courier package arriving in a dusty town, a letter that carried a dream.

'He called it the bellwether of education,' said R. Prasad, who led ICFAI's DLC. Prasad is another IIT-IIM alumnus who made ICFAI their home.

Of Yasaswy, Prasad said, 'He wanted to cater to the average student. Distance learning, to him, wasn't second-rate; it was the future.' Yasaswy believed the classroom neither needed neither four walls nor a clock. What it needed was relevance.

'Outcomes count,' Yasaswy said in a meeting, eyes lighting up. 'When a student is 2,000 kilometres away, the only thing that matters is—did they become better because of us?'

That meeting changed everything. 'We began designing for outcomes, not inputs,' Prasad recalled. 'It wasn't about how smart they were when they joined. It was about what we made them capable of.'

He referred to it as the 'cafeteria model' of learning. 'You chose what you needed. You learnt at your pace. You owned your journey.'

Said Prasad, 'The real outcome wasn't the diploma. It was: can this learner make a difference on the job from day one?

'Yasaswy was a master of communication. Every few weeks, he'd send us updates—what was working, what wasn't. He'd tell us, "There are good and bad things everywhere. But we make ICFAI together."'

That spirit of inclusiveness, of feedback loops, of dualities coexisting, is what gave ICFAI its emotional architecture. 'He encouraged us to be comfortable amidst contradictions,' said R. Prasad. 'That's how institutions last a hundred years.'

When Yasaswy first spoke of learning without walls, the internet didn't exist. When he last spoke of it, India was online. Between those two moments a revolution took place—a man's belief that education, if delivered right, could change not just the student, but a nation.

Prasad distilled Yasaswy's philosophy into three levers. These are lessons that are relevant to every modern university.

First accountability. Growth isn't a department's job; it's a leader's signature. Take ownership of both relevance and reach, for it starts, and ends, with you. Next, locality trap. Don't chase national rankings. Become the thought leader of your region. Make your town smarter, and your brand will follow. Finally, communication. Keep people in the loop. Yasaswy kept everyone informed—what others were doing, what was working, what wasn't. It created belonging.

'Distance,' Prasad said, 'isn't about geography. It's about effort. Of how far an institution is willing to go to reach the learner.'

Chapter 13

Courts of Law; Tests of Will

While ICFAI's couriers carried study material to distant towns, legal summonses were being delivered to Hyderabad. The movement was growing, and so was the resistance.

ICFAI wasn't a university yet, but everything about it—its name, its ambition, even its right to teach—was under scrutiny. From the corridors of ICAI to the courtrooms of Virginia, the resistance began early, and it would continue long after ICFAI became a university.

Fight across Oceans

A document lay on the table, the seal of the US District Court, glinting faintly. Yasaswy read the verdict, his eyes steady.

ICFAI could no longer use the 'CFA' designation in the United States and Canada. The CFA Institute had won its trademark infringement case.

He set the papers down, leaned back, and exhaled.

'We will comply,' he said, adding, 'But let's not lose focus. We move forward.' There was no outburst. Just clarity and a quiet course correction.

To understand the verdict, one had to go back to where it began.

ICFAI's CFA programme was a game-changer in India. It was rigorous, relevant, and had, over the years, become a trusted brand.

In Virginia, that triggered alarms. The CFA Institute alleged trademark infringement.

The first blow came in 1998—a default judgement. ICFAI hadn't even responded, unaware the suit was underway. The court banned using 'CFA' in the US and Canada.

Nearly a decade later, ICFAI returned to court, arguing that the US court lacked jurisdiction because ICFAI had no offices, assets, or advertising in the US.

Judge Leonie M. Brinkema disagreed. She pointed to past Board-level interactions with the CFA Institute. That, she ruled, constituted 'minimum contact'. The ruling declared ICFAI's use of 'CFA' a wilful infringement.

Then came the sting: in 2009, a fine of over $1 million was imposed. For a self-funded Indian institution, that fine could have sunk morale. It didn't.

Yasaswy read every line of that ruling. 'We won't hide from the truth,' he told his Board. 'But we won't surrender our vision either.'

The final settlement came in 2012. Under its terms, ICFAI ceased offering the 'CFA' designation globally; existing holders could use 'CFA (ICFAI)' for clarity; and the CFA Institute retained exclusive global trademark rights.

It was a compromise. But it wasn't a defeat.

Charter vs. Charter

If the global fight was about branding, the domestic one was about identity.

In 1989, the Institute of Chartered Accountants of India (ICAI) notified that any chartered accountant acquiring the

CFA (ICFAI) designation after 1 January 1990 would face disciplinary action for professional misconduct.

Their argument was curious: 'CFA' sounded too much like 'FCA' and could confuse the public.

Yasaswy raised an eyebrow. ICFAI filed a constitutional petition. The notification, they argued, violated fundamental rights.

It took nearly two decades, an entire generation of students waiting in uncertainty, before the judgement came in 2007, and this time, it was in ICFAI's favour. A bench led by Justice S.B. Sinha, which had Justices S.H. Kapadia and B. Sudershan Reddy, struck down the ICAI directive.

Yasaswy didn't gloat. 'Let the learner choose his ladder,' he said. That single line captured his faith in both choice and fairness.

When Students Sued

This next case hit closer to the bone, questioning ICFAI's credibility.

By the late 2000s, the ICFAI National College had grown rapidly, bringing private management education to Tier-2 and Tier-3 towns. And then, the complaints arrived.

Students claimed they had been misled; that the programmes were advertised as nationally recognized degrees when recognition varied from state to state. It wasn't deception; it was friction between scale and compliance.

In 2011, the Delhi State Consumer Disputes Redressal Commission ruled in favour of the students. The verdict cited unclear communication and lack of transparency. In Uttar Pradesh, similar rulings followed, and refunds were ordered.

The ruling hurt. For an institution built on trust, being

told it had failed its students was a deeper wound than any financial penalty.

Inside the Hyderabad office, a senior manager asked Yasaswy, 'Should we appeal?'

He shook his head. 'No. Let's fix what's broken.'

INC was gradually dismantled. Degrees were routed through recognized state universities like ICFAI University, Tripura, and ICFAI University, Dehradun.

Meanwhile, a PIL had been filed against IBS Chennai, challenging ICFAI's right to operate there as a society registered in Andhra Pradesh.

Courts in Delhi, Indore and Jabalpur sided with ICFAI. But in Chennai the case dragged, and IBS pulled out.

Facing The Fire

Most people see courtrooms as battlegrounds. Yasaswy saw them as tests of integrity. He read every court order. Annotated every page.

He didn't resent the CFA Institute. 'They're defending their turf. We'd do the same.' He didn't scorn ICAI. 'Fear makes people overstep. Our job is to be calm, not combative.' He didn't blame the students. 'They trusted us. If they feel misled, that's on us.'

Addressing deans, professors and administrators who had seen the entire arc, he had said, 'We didn't go looking for these fights. But we faced them—with spine, with grace.' Each ruling made ICFAI leaner, sharper and more transparent.

Chapter 14

Certification to Cause

It was late afternoon in Hyderabad. The fan ticked lazily above a teak table stacked with files.

At Dehradun. Something unusual was happening. A bill allowing private universities to be set up through a state act was being discussed.

In Hyderabad, M.V. Siva Ram sat across from N.J. Yasaswy.

'Sir, Uttarakhand may unlock the door,' he said. 'A real university; one that's truly ours.'

Yasaswy leaned forward. 'So, it's possible.'

'Yes. Through the state assembly.'

There was a long pause. Then Yasaswy said quietly, 'This changes everything.'

He looked out the window, already three moves ahead in his mind. If ICFAI could attain university status in one state, what stopped it from doing the same in ten? Why stop at management education when law and engineering beckoned?

'We're not here to be a business school brand,' he told his core team that week. 'We're here to build an education republic.'

❧

The idea of a university wasn't new. Years ago, someone suggested applying for 'Deemed University' status. Yasaswy recoiled.

But as the 2000s dawned, the heat was on. Students wanted degrees that could travel, and parents wanted legitimacy.

Reluctantly, Yasaswy agreed to test the waters.

The UGC inspection team came. Nods were exchanged. The No-Objection Certificate arrived faster. Then came the fine print: every syllabus, every change required Central approval.

'It's not a crown,' Yasaswy told his team. 'It's a leash. And we are not going to be tied to one.' They dropped the idea. But the dream stayed.

ICFAI's first universities didn't rise in metros. Deep in the Northeast, they took root where most others didn't even look.

So how did it begin?

Prof. P.V. Indiresan, former Director of IIT Madras, now ICFAI Board member, had just authored *Vision 2020: What India Can Be, and How to Make That Happen* (2003)—a study of India's educational gaps. He wanted an old friend, President A.P.J. Abdul Kalam, to launch it.

Chairman Besant Raj, Prof. Indiresan, and senior leaders called on the president. Kalam flipped through the book, nodded, and dropped a bomb.

'Reputed institutes like ICFAI should help build educational infrastructure in the Northeast.'

That was it. No directive. A suggestion.

But Yasaswy took it differently. 'The President has served. It's our turn to play,' he said. 'We go first. We go fast.'

And just like that, ICFAI changed its map, pointing not toward Delhi or Mumbai but toward Tripura, Mizoram and Nagaland. The dream had become an itinerary.

The initial breakthrough came from Sikkim.

Siva Ram discovered that Sikkim Manipal University had been established under a state act in 1994. It meant that ICFAI now had a legal doorway.

He flew to Gangtok with a pitch: a world-class private university he argued, one that could attract both jobs and dignity.

The officials nodded and said, 'We already have one private university. Two is a crowd.'

He returned to Hyderabad—disappointed, not defeated.

'If Sikkim won't open the door,' Yasaswy told him, 'we'll knock elsewhere.'

Odisha showed promise, but then politics killed it.

Siva Ram met Chief Minister Naveen Patnaik through an old contact. The meeting, scheduled for fifteen minutes, ran for forty-five. Patnaik liked what he heard. Over the next three nights, ICFAI's team and the state's legal drafters shaped the Odisha Private Universities Bill.

The Cabinet cleared it, but elections were announced before the Assembly could act, and the Bill died.

'A stillborn law,' Yasaswy said softly.

Finally, one afternoon in Hyderabad, while trawling education department websites, Siva Ram found it—Chhattisgarh. A state barely eighteen-months old had a Private University Act and was eager for investment and open to outsiders.

ICFAI filed its application. On 27 September 2002, it was notified as a university.

The joy didn't last.

In 2005, the Supreme Court struck down the Chhattisgarh Private Universities Act. All degrees issued under it were invalidated. Many institutions folded up. ICFAI didn't.

'Don't panic,' Yasaswy told his team. 'We'll find another way.'

They regrouped. Students were shifted. Faculties were consolidated into other locations.

Meanwhile, the Uttarakhand Bill was on life support.

The Opposition wanted it killed. Enter Dr M. Ramachandran, IAS. He visited every MLA, one by one. One signature at a time, he kept the dream breathing. And presto, the Bill was passed.

In 2003, ICFAI University, Dehradun, was born. Officially, it was ICFAI's second university, but with the scrapping of Chhattisgarh, it is today the first under the ICFAI belt!

State by state, like a man on a mission, Siva Ram criss-crossed India. Each visit meant new paperwork and new resistance.

Tripura came next.

Biplab Haider, yet another IIT-IIM alumnus, spearheaded the initiative. Conversations with the chief and law secretaries did the trick. The Bill was cleared in six months.

While Biplab built foundations in Tripura, Siva Ram moved fast across the Northeast. Nagaland followed. Then Mizoram. It took multiple meetings, intense negotiations, and a personal pitch to the chief minister to finally clear the Act.

Meghalaya was the trickiest. ICFAI was told to build a campus and then come back for legislation there. It meant taking a leap—investing crores without legal cover. ICFAI took the risk. It paid off.

Then came Sikkim. One signature stood between the Bill and the law. The chief minister's.

The man was sixty kilometres away, deep in the hills, unreachable by phone. That night, Yasaswy got the update. He didn't ask questions; he just said, 'If the mountain won't come to us…'

At dawn, after a sleepless drive through misty bends and blind turns, the team caught up with the chief minister, just as he was stepping out for tea.

They made their pitch. He listened, nodded and signed.

And just like that, ICFAI University, Sikkim was born—in a mountain town, over a cup of tea, before the fog rolled back in.

By 2006, six ICFAI universities were in place. By 2011, there were eleven. Each was set up under a state Act, with not a rupee from the Centre. In Yasaswy's language, this was the federal model: 'a decentralized grid of universities, each with its own Act, Board, and Vice-Chancellor.'

All of this happened because one man, Yasaswy, dared to dream. Another, Siva Ram, dared to chase. And builders like Biplab dared to stay the course—with Yasaswy's voice in their ears the whole way.

Trial in Tripura

The call came late in the evening.

'I've been told they've asked you to go to Tripura,' Yasaswy said.

J.J. Kawle nodded.

That morning, he had quietly pulled out a map and scanned the northeastern part of India. There it was—Tripura. Remote. Unfamiliar. And now, Yasaswy was asking him to go build a university there.

'You don't have to commit to anything. Go there. Stay for fifteen days. If you don't like it, feel free to come back. Your position here is safe.'

That one sentence changed everything. Kawle took the flight.

When he landed in Agartala, it felt less like an assignment and more like being parachuted into another planet.

On Day Two, he was taken to the chief minister's office to meet the personal assistant. A vague assurance of help was offered. 'No instructions. No handover.' Kawle recalls. 'I was supposed to start an engineering college from scratch by April.'

It was December. It meant there were just about 120 days to go.

An administrative officer, Subhash Ghosh, was assigned to him. They located an old land-survey training institute on the city's edge. Dusty, forgotten, abandoned, but available. He walked through broken windows and peeling paint, imagining classrooms where cobwebs hung!

Ads were placed. Phone calls made. Trips to Guwahati and Shillong followed. Within three months, they had recruited five young, eager faculty members.

'And when we opened,' Kawle says, 'we had eight students.' Just eight hopeful students and five teachers believed in a university.

What made Kawle stay was the 'challenge'. 'Everything had to be created from nothing. No resources, no connections, no blueprint. That made it irresistible.' What anchored him was Yasaswy. He didn't hover. He enabled it.

As the number of students grew, the next challenge loomed: land acquisition. Eventually, a plot was found—thirty-five acres with twenty-seven different owners. Through negotiation, persuasion, and patience, they closed the deal.

When it was time to lay the foundation stone, they invited Chief Minister, Manik Sarkar. Known for his austere lifestyle, he declined. 'I've laid too many foundation stones that became graveyards.'

Two years later, when the campus stood gleaming, they went back to Sarkar. This time, he came willingly. 'You're the only group,' he said, 'that delivered what it promised.'

Tripura was only the beginning. Over the next six years, Kawle led the charge across the Northeast: Mizoram, Meghalaya, Nagaland and Sikkim.

For each state the same brief was given—start in a rented building, recruit faculty, convince parents, acquire land, build a campus, and stay the course.

Tripura showed what vision could do when paired

with will. When he finally stepped away in 2012, the Northeast had gone from being a blank patch on ICFAI's map to a necklace of functioning universities.

When critics questioned the logic of investing in the Northeast, citing poor infrastructure, rugged terrain, and lack of talent, Yasaswy had only one line: 'That's why we must go. There are no resources? That means there's opportunity. We start from zero. And we build.'

Today, those once-remote campuses now contribute significantly to ICFAI's financials. Clearly, persistence compounds.

Ten state private universities. One deemed university. But behind every statute and site plan was a question Yasaswy kept asking: what will endure?

Eight Hundred Years Ahead

Cameras whirred. The projector flickered. The microphone clicked, and the room fell silent.

N.J. Yasaswy stepped forward. He looked out at the audience. Some were his colleagues, and others were outsiders—academicians, potential allies. They had come expecting a talk, but what they got was a vision.

'Eight hundred years.'

He let it hang.

'Eight hundred years is a long time. I'll be gone. You'll be gone. The mobile phone will be gone. Even Google. But guess what will remain? Oxford. Cambridge. Harvard. And if we get this right—us.'

A ripple of laughter broke the tension.

Yasaswy smiled. 'Some of you think that I am mad. You're not wrong. Every great vision starts with a little madness.'

He continued, 'We're not here to build just another university. We're here to build a university where academia, industry and India unite to solve problems that matter.

'We won't just create knowledge. We'll turn it into action. Because any learning that doesn't lead to action,' he said, grinning, 'is like that treadmill in your living room. Looks expensive. Burns nothing.

'Some of you still wonder, "Why can't we just be good? Why aim for the top hundred in the world?" Let me ask you. Do you want to be good? Or do you want to be great? Greatness isn't ego. It's a responsibility. Because scale creates impact, and impact drives transformation.'

A slide lit up behind him—campuses, labs, satellites, green rooftops.

'By 2030, this is what we build: tens of thousands of students, world-class research labs, and fifty global university partnerships. A university so vital to India's innovation economy that people can't imagine India without it.'

He brought his hands together in a triangle, his signature gesture. 'Yes, I know it's ambitious. But you're not dreaming big enough if your dreams don't scare you.'

He glanced at the screen. 'Let me show you something—a precedent. Stanford. In just hundred and twenty years, it went from a regional campus to the birthplace of Silicon Valley. Google, Yahoo!, Cisco—all born there. Trillions in value. All from one institution. So why not us?'

You could hear a pin drop.

'Take Harvard. It is four hundred years old. It gave the world seven US Presidents and thousands of scientists, CEOs, Nobel laureates, and Fortune 500 leaders. What if we built an Indian university like that? One that produced visionaries who shape industries, shape countries.'

He stepped forward, voice rising.

'We have one billion minds. Why should we import ambition? Let's create disruptors. People who don't just complain about potholes but fix them. And then patent the solution.'

He chuckled.

'We don't need more followers. We need entrepreneurial thinkers in every field. Start-ups. Schools. Hospitals. Courts. We need Idea Entrepreneurs.

'When I was in college, it took me six months to find the address of a professional institute. There was no internet. No direction. I could've said, "The system failed me." But I didn't. I figured it out.

'At ASCI, I learned something else. Professionals don't want lectures. They want action. And the best leaders don't complain about the rules. They succeed despite them.

'That's what this is about. When discussing a university that lasts eight hundred years, I'm not talking about waiting for the perfect environment. I'm talking about building right now with what we have.

'I've seen CEOs thrive in red tape. And I've seen what's possible when people stop waiting and start doing.'

He scanned the room. 'If we commit to this idea—an institution without boundaries—then no force on earth can stop us.'

He paused.

'And here's the thing. This isn't my dream. It's our collective responsibility. If we want to stand tall eight hundred years from now, we must start today.'

He smiled. 'And if that doesn't move you… think about your name on a building eight hundred years from now. Not bad, right?'

He pressed forward.

'Here's what we aim for in the next fifty years: fifty international collaborations. Research centres that solve real problems. One university in every Indian state capital. One free school in every state because no child should be held back by their wallet. And yes, we will break into the top fifty global rankings.'

Someone called out, 'Why fifty?'

He grinned. 'Because I was born in 1950.'

Then he locked eyes with the audience. 'This isn't about rankings. It's about impact. About changing families. Our politicians have failed us, but we must not forget India.'

He paused for a moment.

'This won't be easy. The greatest institutions were never built in comfort. They were built by mavericks, held together by grit, and sustained by those who refused to give up.'

He picked up a glass of water. It had been left untouched. 'And by people who sit through an entire speech without drinking from this.'

Laughter echoed. Then quiet again.

'Some eight hundred years from now, the world may not remember us, but they will remember what we built. Stanford and Harvard did it. Now is our turn.'

The room erupted. Cameras flashed. Some clapped, others simply stared—because belief takes a moment to set in.

Backstage, a journalist asked him, 'Do you think it worked?'

Yasaswy smiled. 'If five per cent of them believe...this hour was worth it.'

Hours later, long after the crowd had left and the lights were switched off, the auditorium still glowed.

Chapter 15

When Law Met Tech

If you run a university, you must broad-base your offerings. Beyond management, one must look at engineering, law, medicine, and arts and science.

When N.J. Yasaswy walked into the faculty lounge at BITS Pilani that morning, the professors didn't know what to expect. He wasn't an engineer. He didn't come with a doctorate. But the moment he started to speak, heads turned in his direction.

Yasaswy had come with an unusual ask.

He laid out a clear and bold blueprint. 'We don't want to build another engineering college,' he said. 'We want to build engineers who can code, think, speak, and lead.' It was the kind of line that invited attention.

There was something about the way he spoke. Measured but firm. He carried the weight of having built something before. IBS had already proven what was possible when vision met execution. Now, he was asking the engineers to help him build a new tech institution, from scratch.

Among those listening was Dr G.P. Srivastava, a senior professor and thirty-five-year veteran at BITS. Later, he would reflect, 'We expected a conversation. He unveiled a prototype.'

Yasaswy hadn't come alone. Seated beside him was Dr V. Panduranga Rao, an economics professor who had once walked these corridors and later helped Yasaswy shape the IBS model.

Most people sought association. Yasaswy offered a challenge—and a cheque. 'He didn't want to borrow our brand,' one faculty member said later. He wanted to borrow our brains, and was willing to pay for it.' That clarity of intent turned the meeting into a collaboration.

Soon, a curriculum committee was formed. Dr Maheshwari, Dr Patnaik, and Dr Srivastava were brought on board as consultants. The discussions that followed were intense. And then it had to be implemented.

The ground reality was less inspiring.

The selected site was Suchitra, a dusty patch on the fringes of Hyderabad. A stray dog watched them from a distance. Standing there with a rolled-up blueprint, Dr Saini wasn't sure whether he was witnessing vision or volunteering for madness. Beside him, Yasaswy surveyed the land in silence before speaking in his usual, low-key tone. 'No shortcuts,' he said. 'Faculty, labs, curriculum—everything must be right. This isn't a brand launch. This is a legacy.'

By 2002, the first campuses opened in Hyderabad and Bhubaneswar. Not long after, Jaipur, Bangalore, Dehradun and Bhilai followed. Yasaswy wasn't building a single institution. He was setting up a multi-campus, multi-state tech university that focused not on prestige but on preparation.

The operating model was different. Every ICFAI Tech student had to complete two internships —a shorter stint after their second year and a longer, five-month final project in their fourth. These were industry assignments, evaluated jointly by external professionals and internal faculty, and counted towards the final grades.

Electives ranged from biotechnology to economics to literature. Dual degrees were on the table for those interested.

Faculty hiring had its own filter. 'Passion first, qualifications second,' Yasaswy would say. He offered a blunt test: 'If they can't teach like their life depends on it, don't hire them, because the students' lives do.'

The students didn't arrive with JEE ranks in the top one per cent. Many came from small towns, others from middle-class. But they showed up hungry, worked hard, and often left transformed.

ICFAI Tech didn't pretend to be the first-choice brand; it wasn't meant to. Yasaswy focused on rethinking engineering education, turning it from theory-heavy to industry-ready. Engineering was a field choked with regulation and plagued by poor finishing quality. It was precisely that challenge that drew him in.

Then came the tsunami. Literally.

In December 2004, the Indian Ocean earthquake triggered one of the worst natural disasters. At ICFAI Tech, a group of students watched the coverage unfold on TV. Screens flickered blue as waves swallowed towns. But instead of stopping at grief, they rolled up their sleeves. Over the next few weeks, they designed a tsunami early warning system—a working prototype submitted to an IEEE-Microsoft global competition.

Entries poured in from all over the world. ICFAI Tech made the final ten. Four students, most of whom had never flown abroad, presented their work in Washington, D.C. They walked away with a $4,000 prize and, more importantly, a belief that they belonged.

When Dr Srivastava called Yasaswy to inform about this accomplishment he said, 'Tell them this is like winning the Oscars.'

Around this time, the real challenge arrived. This time from the courts.

In 2008–09, engineering students in Hyderabad and Bangalore began protesting. They had realized that their degrees were being issued by the university in Dehradun. While it was legally sound, it felt wrong to them. Competitors fanned the flames.

The Vice Chancellor of Dehradun stepped down, and the protests escalated. In response, Yasaswy didn't issue memos or stage town halls. Instead, he picked up the phone.

'G.P., we need you.'

Dr Srivastava had just retired. He was asked to take charge, rework the structure, shut down state campuses without university charters, relocate a thousand and six hundred students—all without losing a single academic year.

Through all of it, the core model remained. Internships continued. Labs stayed real. Electives stayed wide-ranging. Industry evaluations were on. Faculty hiring standards didn't drop. The system was bending but not breaking.

By 2010, ICFAI Tech had active campuses in Hyderabad, Dehradun, Jaipur, Ranchi, Tripura, Raipur and Himachal. It hadn't become a household name but it had become a home for thousands.

Yasaswy was once asked why he entered the crowded world of engineering education when IBS could have scaled faster and farther elsewhere.

His answer was characteristically simple: 'Because someone had to, and I couldn't wait for them.'

Today, over ten thousand students study under the ICFAI Tech umbrella. Their stories don't always make headlines but they're proof that second-choice students, given first-class systems, can do world-class things.

More Than a Law School

Revolutions don't always start in courtrooms. Sometimes, they start over coffee. It began with a question Yasaswy tossed casually across a table.

'Why do we see lawyers solely as case-fighters?' In that room of senior academics, the question stirred reflection.

Nobody responded. It was the early 2000s. India's economy was racing ahead, powered by a new breed of entrepreneurs, cross-border deals, and a thousand-page contract culture. Every boardroom had a lawyer on speed dial to avoid court fights.

'We don't need courtroom warriors,' Yasaswy said with confidence. 'We need legal minds who walk with business leaders, not behind them. People who prevent fires from happening, not firefighters who come while the fire is on.'

The man seated diagonally across from him blinked. He'd seen this before. The quiet tone. The measured pace. And then, boom, the blueprint.

'What if we created a different kind of law school?' Yasaswy asked, almost talking to himself. 'One that builds not just lawyers, but legal strategists.'

'BBA LLB?' someone offered.

He nodded, but his mind was racing ahead. 'Exactly. And why stop there? Criminal Law. Intellectual Property (IP). The economy is transforming. Our legal education should, too.'

That was how it started.

In 2003, the idea of a five-year integrated law programme wasn't revolutionary in India. The National Law Universities (NLUs) were already doing it well. But Yasaswy wasn't competing; he was completing what they couldn't cover.

Another day, he said, 'NLUs are good. But there aren't enough seats. And they train for the court. I want to train for the boardroom.'

To him, a great lawyer wasn't someone who won in court. It was someone who kept you out of court. He said, 'We need legal thinkers who understand business.'

He sketched the law school idea on a whiteboard: three columns and three categories.

First, the interpreters. These in-house legal minds could read a contract and say, 'This clause will cost you ten crore in two years.' Next, the courtroom warriors. Those who mastered constitutional and other laws and stepped into a courtroom to fight. Finally, the IP experts. With India's entry into the knowledge race, lawsuits over patents, trademarks, and digital theft would explode. Who was training for that?

Yasaswy tapped the board. 'This isn't just law. This is strategy. And strategy needs structure.' He turned to his team and said, almost mischievously, 'We don't just need lawyers who can speak business. We need MBAs who can speak legally.'

That philosophy became a programme.

It introduced a five-year BBA LLB, a fusion of business and law. Later, BA LLB and even BCJ LLB, a first-of-its-kind programme combining journalism and law, followed in nine campuses. Nine times the paperwork.

The law schools didn't just teach case law. They lived it. Legal aid clinics sprang up in the neighbourhood. At Shankarpally, students sat under banyan trees, helping villagers untangle land issues and pension paperwork.

Then came the moot courts. Judges arrived from real benches, and students argued like their scholarships depended on it. IAS officers were invited for guest talks. Law firm partners conducted workshops. Even journalists and IFS officers joined the discussions.

Faculty retention was unusually high.

'Some of our professors have been with us for ten to fifteen years,' a senior head said. 'That doesn't happen unless there's purpose.'

Yasaswy had a rule when starting a new programme: hire the faculty first, build the infrastructure next, and finally admit students. He preferred a quiet build-up. But when the doors opened, everything was ready.

He was building a law school without ever entering a courtroom. 'Law is too important a subject for it to be designed by lawyers alone' appeared to be his credo.

In setting up the law schools, Yasaswy knew India would need people who understood rules, not just those who could argue them. He was training the architects of compliance; the lawyers who'd keep the system honest by design, not defence. And somewhere, in the corridors of ICFAI Law School, you can almost hear him say: 'Build institutions that prevent the fire, not the ones that fight it.'

Chapter 16

A 'Case' of Coming Good

It was 1998. Internet cafés still whirred on dial-up. N.J. Yasaswy got himself a Harvard case just to see what the fuss was about. 'What if,' Yasaswy wondered, 'we built our own Harvard here in Hyderabad?'

The idea seemed laughable. A private Indian institution entering the elite world of global business case writing? That world belonged to America's Harvard, France's INSEAD, and Switzerland's IMD (International Institute for Management Development).

But Yasaswy wasn't interested in fitting in. He was there to rewrite the rulebook. For the nth time, he was playing the role of an upstart doing what the superstars wouldn't. For him, the classroom was a lab of adaptation.

Harvard's case method was designed for the blazer-sporting MBAs of Boston. Yasaswy wanted to bring the same to the pyjama-kurta-clad kids in Indian classrooms. As Sanjib Dutta, who currently heads the Case initiative, says, 'There was a dearth of case studies dealing with Indian businesses, and Yasaswy saw in this an opportunity to adapt the Harvard model in the Indian context.'

But who would craft these cases? Us, he decided without hesitation.

The journey began modestly in the late 1990s with

A.V. Vedpuriswar writing twenty-page to twenty-five-page case studies on Fortune 500 Companies. He was later joined by Naveen Das and S.S. George. Sanjib joined in 1999 as Faculty Associate at ITUC Transworld University School of Management, reporting to Ved, who was Dean.

ICFAI Center for Management Research (ICMR) was established in the early 2000s. Due to tensions with the CFA Institute in the US, ICMR was soon rebranded as the IBS Center for Management Research. After moving to the university campus, the Center was named the IBS Case Research Centre (CRC) in 2010.

What began as a tiny unit became, over the next twenty-five years, ICFAI's crown jewel. When visitors turn up in Hyderabad, a visit to CRC is mandatory. The centre may well be Yasaswy's most enduring legacy—a Harvard of the East built quietly in India's South.

When it all began, a team of fewer than twenty researchers sat in a small room, sifting through old issues of *Business India* and *The Hindu Business Line*. The internet had just arrived, and resources at the Institute were slim. The industry wasn't falling over itself to offer interviews.

So Yasaswy worked a way out. If the team couldn't do primary research, so be it. They would do secondary research. These are known as library cases. The know-alls mocked it as ruthless exploitation of the internet. They sneered: 'Ctrl + C, Ctrl + V Centre'. But Yasaswy smiled.

'He didn't care a jot,' recalls Prof. P. Indu. 'He never saw constraints. He only saw the runway.'

They began as essays about Fortune 500 companies but over time became intellectually sharp and narratively rich.

Each case was stitched with research, analysis, and narrative tension. They were written to simulate real decisions. Acquisitions, layoffs, leadership calls, innovation dilemmas—everything came in.

In a good year, the team produced a hundred and fifty full-length teaching cases. Each case took four to eight weeks to develop.

And Yasaswy? He was never far from the details. No, he wasn't hovering over keyboards or distributing checklists. Yet every writer knew he was watching as a mentor.

'Sometimes, he'd scribble a line on a piece of paper,' Prof. P. Debapratim said. 'He would ask, "What keeps the CEO awake at night?" That became our North Star.'

'This was the Socratic method, resurrected,' Indu said. 'You weren't told what to think. You were asked, "What would you do if you were the CEO?"'

And slowly, the world began to notice.

Five years later, the first ripples appeared on the global radar.

In 2003, a few CRC cases were quietly placed in ECCH—the European Case Clearing House, now The Case Centre. Orders trickled in and then flowed.

In 2006, McKinsey ordered a case. Other biggies followed.

That same year, ICFAI was placed second at Canada's prestigious John Molson International Case Writing Competition. The West had noticed. From Hyderabad, the echo reached Harvard's corridors. In a later year, the legendary Harvard picked several copies.

Suddenly, global classrooms debated Fortune 500 boardroom dramas drafted by writers half a world away. The centre of gravity was tilting east.

Soon, the CRC faculty started conducting workshops both in India and overseas: at TAPMI and IIM Bangalore, California, Vancouver and Philadelphia.

While the West continued to write about Western strategy, ICFAI went after emerging markets. Indian companies—Infosys, Tata, Flipkart, Café Coffee Day—were case models. Each year, roughly thirty to forty per cent of ICFAI's cases focused on Indian firms.

The revenue model was interesting. When a professor handled a case, he had to buy one for each student. If there were sixty students, he bought sixty copies. Xeroxing wasn't allowed.

Every purchase was proof that someone somewhere was learning from a story written by a young mind in Hyderabad.

Yasaswy helped CRC see what was coming. He would suggest topics months before they hit the headlines—airline mergers, corporate scandals, cross-border acquisitions. 'Write about that,' he'd say. The team would do that, and the world would read. He saw trends before anyone else felt the pull.

When trends shifted to digital formats, CRC adapted. A few cases were written like Netflix episodes—racy and punchy. Others were mini-series: three to five instances tracking a company's evolution.

As the reputation soared, so did the quality of the audience. The readers weren't just MBA students anymore. They included Fortune 500 Vice Presidents.

Slowly, CRC's reach expanded. Georgia Institute of Technology, Arizona State University, and UCLA frequently featured them in the US. LSE, London Business School, Oxford, and Cambridge became buyers in the UK.

The awards kept coming. In a *Financial Times* article titled 'How real-world cases work as business school teaching tools,' a case written by CRC was quoted as one of the Top Ten Cases. Three of the global top five bestselling authors are from ICFAI.

Yasaswy didn't micromanage. He nudged. He trusted his writers, even those from unconventional backgrounds. Indu was one such writer. She came from banking and logistics, had no PhD and never worked in academia. S.S. George trained her and demanded excellence. 'George was ruthless,' she admitted. 'But he built our foundation.'

In 2010, the case-writing unit was integrated into the larger university system. What began as separate cells for talent now fused into a single powerhouse. Output soared. Operationally, it made sense. However, several senior writers moved on because the campus was far from the city, and commuting was time-consuming.

By 2015, according to The Case Research Centre data, ICFAI was ranked among the top five case-producing institutions in the world, competing with over three hundred institutions. Without an Ivy League sheen, it had muscled its way into the front row, with consistent, world-class output.

In 2015, P. Debapratim received the Lifetime Achievement Award for Outstanding Contribution to the Case Method.

By 2025, twenty-five years after its birth, ICFAI's CRC ranked just below Harvard in global impact—measured by classroom adoption worldwide. Yes, Harvard still topped the charts. But right beneath that, in bold on that list, was a name few outside India could pronounce: ICFAI.

What A.V. Vedpuriswar began around 1998 and what Naveen Das and S.S. George had carried forward was now seeing fruition.

The real recognition came from the class rosters. That was the genuine applause—when ideas became discussions in classrooms worldwide. Classics like McKinsey's Knowledge Management, Zara's Supply Chain, and Tata's JLR Acquisition became textbook material.

So were 'Knowledge Management Practices at Toyota Motors', 'Netflix: Leveraging Big Data to Predict Entertainment Hits', and 'IKEA in Russia: Ethical Dilemmas Cases', which were written fifteen years ago and continued to sell year after year.

What started as Yasaswy's conviction, that students must read about Indian cases, may not have happened, but cases written in India did!

PART V

Walking Together

If you want to go fast, go alone.
If you want to go far, go together.

—AFRICAN PROVERB

Chapter 17

Across the Table

These weren't hires. They were independent thinkers who sat across from him as equals, helping his relentless intellect shape an institution. He built through conversations.

Let's travel to Hyderabad, 1974.

Dr J. Mahender Reddy first heard the name in a coffee room at ASCI. 'That's N.J. Yasaswy. Just twenty-four but brilliant,' someone said.

It didn't take Dr Reddy long to see for himself. Yasaswy's sessions on 'Finance for Non-Finance Executives' were packed. He provoked questions and offered unmatched insights.

'I knew,' Dr Reddy would later say, 'he was destined for bigger things.'

In 2002, Yasaswy invited Dr Reddy back into his orbit. 'Can you join as Principal and teach in our ICFAI Institute for Management Teachers (IIMT)?' he asked.

Reddy agreed, and a new phase began between the teacher and his former prodigy, now collaborators.

Yasaswy chaired every meeting and pushed hard for visiting scholars, research clusters, and faculty-led content. 'He wasn't just running a university. He was building a culture.'

In 2009, Dr Reddy became Vice Chancellor of ICFAI University, Hyderabad. Campus reviews with Yasaswy turned into daylong marathons—from curriculum design to hostel plumbing.

Reddy may have joined early, but he wasn't alone. Across boardrooms, others too were drawn into his orbit.

The Professor and the Papaya

In 1985, at Taj Banjara, Yasaswy met Prof. V. Raghunathan of IIM Ahmedabad in the quiet corner of a coffee shop. He was laying the foundations for ICFAI and had reached out to the popular professor.

'I'd like you to join the Board of Academic Advisors,' he said.

That first conversation sparked a professional alliance built on respect, curiosity, and humour. They met regularly, and the discussions were always stimulating.

One morning, Yasaswy invited the professor for breakfast. 'Come home,' he said. 'Papaya and honey are compulsory.'

Raghunathan agreed.

Sobharani, Yasaswy's wife, played the perfect co-host. Forgotten Andhra recipes lined the table, the air rich with ghee and conversation.

'Spending an hour with him,' Raghunathan says, 'was like reading a good book.'

The man had a way of asking deceptive questions: 'Is ambition always selfish?' He would wait as you searched for an answer. Just when you thought you were cornered, he'd answer by drawing on anecdotes, philosophy and humour. He could slip from Aristotle to Arthashastra without losing the thread.

Over the years, their association deepened. Raghunathan moved on to ING Vysya Bank and GMR Foundation but the rhythm of those early conversations stayed with him. 'He could do high finance at noon and speak of ancient poetry by tea.'

The Strategist from Satyam

We shift to 2000. India's tech industry was on the rise, and CEOs in Hyderabad began dreaming of scale.

Ramalinga Raju had just placed a $125 million bet on a business school. It would be called the Satyam Institute of E-Business. Yasaswy was part of the visioning team, and so was Prof. Kavil Ramachandran.

At one meeting, the topic of the Dean's role came up. Should it go to a seasoned academic?

Yasaswy paused and said, 'The Dean will be a non-academic.' Then he continued, 'Of course, the person must have academic brilliance and deep respect for scholarship. But more than anything, he must be a leader, not just a professor.'

It was pure Yasaswy—turning tradition on its head, yet never losing respect for it.

During Onam, the Ramachandrans invited Yasaswy and Sobharani home for a traditional Kerala feast. The food was served on banana leaves. At the end came a bowl of *pal payasam*.

Yasaswy took a spoonful, paused, and said: 'Divine.'

That one word opened the floodgates. From payasam, the conversation leapt to Parashurama, matrilineal traditions, temple economies, and Kerala's storied spice routes. Yasaswy's knowledge was startling.

'He spoke like someone who had lived there in another life.'

Across three decades, Dr Reddy, Prof. Raghunathan and Prof. Ramachandran each discovered the same thing: sitting across from N.J. Yasaswy wasn't about admiration—it was about ignition.

He didn't hire them. He sparked them.

Many more collaborators and co-creators would follow—drawn by the sheer electricity of an idea taking form. They helped him build ICFAI.

Chapter 18

They Built Beside Him

Institutions aren't built by vision alone. They're built by people who rise to match that vision. This is the story of two such men: one who took the first leap, and another who carried the flame. One left the comfort of a secure job to chase an idea. The other arrived years later, armed with Army discipline and an institution-builder's instinct. One helped launch the institution. The other helped expand it across the country. Different journeys. Same trust.

First Believer

Before there were campuses and case studies, there was one man who said 'Yes.' We begin with the story of the first believer.

A soft-spoken engineer at BHEL, Subhash Sarnikar stunned his colleagues by resigning from his secure public sector job. He bid goodbye to government pay, seniority and pension as he threw his hat into the ring drawn by N.J. Yasaswy.

'I didn't join a company,' Sarnikar says now. 'I joined a vision.'

He became ICFAI's first official employee and stayed there for twenty-five years, through thick and thin, and everything in between.

'Working with Yasaswy felt like entering a relay race already in motion. You'd walk into a meeting to give an update and leave with three new responsibilities. He wasn't like the others,' Sarnikar recalls. 'Most leaders ask, "Can we do this?" Yasaswy asked, "Why haven't we done this?"

'He never threw you into the sea to test you,' Sarnikar adds. 'He threw you in because he believed you'd swim.' He trusted people, but tracked progress. Every day, he sat through five to six review meetings. Every week, he checked academic content: textbooks, case studies and test banks. Every month, he reviewed divisional performance reports. And every day, he monitored cash flows—like a hawk with a calculator.

'We were building ICFAI on a shoestring,' Sarnikar says. 'There were no sugar daddies. Every rupee came from operations and was recycled into the next initiative.'

One of Yasaswy's golden rules was simple. 'Run your division your way,' he'd say, 'but don't ask for a bailout. Create value or course-correct.'

When trouble brewed, Yasaswy didn't blink. When cash flow was tight, he doubled down and found a way. And if something he backed didn't work, he shut it without sentiment. The Securities Research Centre was one of his pet projects. When it failed to deliver, he closed it with the same clarity with which he had once greenlit it.

'He didn't cling to the past,' Sarnikar says. 'If it didn't serve the mission, it didn't survive.' He believed in innovation but never romanticized it.

For Yasaswy, success wasn't applause. It was impact. He didn't scale ICFAI to build an empire. He scaled it to widen access.

Behind the scale was solid scaffolding: discipline, systems, review, and a belief that education should always be win-win.

Perhaps the clearest window into his heart was the IFCAI Republic School. Built for underprivileged children, it offered full-time, quality education at no cost. Uniforms, books, meals—everything was covered. 'Excellence needn't be elitist,' he told the team. 'Talent blooms anywhere, in slums and gullies included.'

Over twenty-five years, Subhash Sarnikar watched it all: the booms, the course corrections, the misfires, and the rebounds. He watched Yasaswy choose frugality over funding, systems over shortcuts, and conviction over conformity.

He rose from being IFCAI's executive director to its chancellor and was Yasaswy's go-to man. And in between he joined and cleared the CFA!

He was, in every sense, the first believer.

The Colonel Yasaswy Trusted

It was the summer of 1999. A retired army officer walked into an interview room full of doctorates. Colonel V.R.K. Prasad had no teaching credentials. But Yasaswy didn't blink.

They spoke, man to man. No resumé reviews.

A few minutes later, Yasaswy made the offer. Prasad liked it but couldn't commit immediately—he had unfinished duties.

Yasaswy didn't push. He simply waited. That was his way: decisive when needed and patient when it mattered.

Almost a year later, on 30 March 2000, Col. Prasad joined ICFAI—not as a teacher but as Manager, Academic Coordination.

Back then, IBS Hyderabad ran out of Building 53 at Nagarjuna Hills. There were three classrooms upstairs and a patchy library downstairs.

'In that hot Hyderabad summer,' Prasad recalled students saying, "Sir, there's no fan! No air conditioner!"

But the academic calendar waited for no one. Within

weeks, the Class of 2000 graduated. IBS Hyderabad had two batches, one full-time faculty member and Prasad running the academic coordination.

Classes ran on grit and borrowed time. But grit wasn't scalable. As student intake surged, infrastructure cracked under pressure.

A second centre opened in Banjara Hills.

'One year,' Prasad said, 'I had to divide the batch into eleven sections. From A to K!'

Every month, Yasaswy reviewed with surgical calm. Action items, pending tasks, and future targets.

He was tough, no doubt. But in return, he offered something rare: he gave people a chance to rise. By 2001, Prasad was promoted to Associate Dean. In 2002, when *Outlook* magazine ranked IBS Hyderabad 31st in the country, Yasaswy didn't celebrate. He raised the bar:

'Let's get to the Top Ten. In five years.'

They got there by 2005. That same year, ICFAI acquired hundred acres of land in Shankarpally.

He called Prasad.

'You'll lead the construction.'

'Sir, I'm not an engineer.'

'You're an Army officer. And a decisive manager. That's what I need. You're now also Director of Projects.'

'I told him I'd do my best. I wouldn't let his trust down.'

The next six years were a blur. Fourteen campuses were under construction. Land was acquired in over twenty cities. Contractors piled in. Budgets stretched.

Prasad was on the road ten to fifteen days a month. Along the way, he developed diabetes, but he kept going. Yasaswy never micromanaged. He asked hard questions. He offered clarity. And then he stepped back.

Sometimes, buildings changed midstream. A shopping

centre became an HR school. A management block became a law school. 'These weren't design errors,' Prasad said. 'We adapted, improvised and delivered.'

In the Northeast, the job felt like a military deployment. There were extortion threats, parallel tax regimes, and civic unrest, but Yasaswy never flinched. 'Education must go where it's needed most,' he often said. Campuses came up in Tura, Agartala, Dimapur, Guwahati.

Elsewhere, delays took other forms—Bhubaneswar stalled over water; Ranchi battled freak weather; Guwahati saw unrest; and Chennai paused due to skyrocketing real estate.

But Yasaswy didn't lose his temper. He recalibrated the scope and trimmed timelines but never compromised the mission. He spent money wisely. Most cities skipped hostels to fund classrooms, faculty, and curriculum. Only Agartala and Hyderabad were exceptions.

Once, SEBI co-hosted an international conference at the Taj Lands End, Mumbai. Yasaswy turned to Prasad.

'You're in charge.'

'Sir, I've no background in finance.'

'That's okay. You don't need a PhD to run this show. You need discipline. You have it.'

Prasad ran the event like a military drill—training students, managing logistics, and rehearsing every move.

When Yasaswy discovered that the student anchors were IBS kids and not professionals, he was stunned.

'They're our students?' he asked wide-eyed. Then smiled. 'Well done.'

Praise from him was rare. And unforgettable. At one packed meeting, he pointed to Prasad and said: 'His claims are so frugal, the finance team wonders how he even completed the assignment.'

Prasad folded his hands. Tears welled up in his eyes.

When Prasad was promoted to Dean, Yasaswy said only this: 'The sincerity you bring—I find it rare.'

They had a weekly rhythm. Prasad would walk into Yasaswy's office with a diary and ten bullet points. They would tick them off, one by one.

'This habit,' Yasaswy said once, 'is worth emulating.'

'It's from my Army days, Sir.'

At one review, Prasad spoke up. 'Sir, we're opening too many colleges—Cygnus, Meritum, Mentoris. We need to consolidate.' Within a year, those institutions were shut down.

In 2006, as the chorus grew to shift IBS to the new campus, Prasad raised his hand. 'Sir, it's not ready. We won't manage this semester. We'll be chasing a mirage.'

The move was postponed.

Under Yasaswy's wing, Prasad transformed. He earned a PhD, wrote books, and trained students across Sri Lanka. But none of that moved him more than one simple sentence from his mentor: 'Ever since I gave him charge of Projects,' Yasaswy once told a visitor, 'I sleep peacefully.'

Years later, when Prasad became Chancellor of ICFAI Nagaland, he honoured his mentor in the only way he knew.

He named three academic blocks N, J and Y. 'They'll remain,' he said, 'as long as the university stands.'

From Nagarjuna Hills to Nagaland, the names may change, but the imprint remains—Yasaswy's. This is the story of a man who placed his trust wisely, and of the men who honoured that trust by turning it into a legacy.

Chapter 19

Prime Movers

Some relationships don't begin with fanfare. One began with a quiet idea: run nine business schools as one. Another started with a rescue mission: revive a sinking campus in Mumbai. What linked them was N.J. Yasaswy and a single currency, viz., trust. In two people, he found men who were unafraid to push limits. Together, these prime movers, Panduranga Rao and Y.K. Bhushan, turned improbable ideas into enduring institutions.

Professor Meets Founder

It was meant to be a routine academic visit. But less than an hour into their first conversation, something clicked.

Panduranga Rao, the economics professor from BITS Pilani, saw 'speed without shallowness'. Yasaswy, the visitor, saw something rarer still: a mind that could turn abstract vision into structured execution.

They made no promises. What began as an exchange of ideas quietly became one of ICFAI's most consequential partnerships.

A few months later, when ICFAI Business School was taking shape, Yasaswy reached out. He was setting up a single business school spread across eight cities, delivering the same programme with the same standards. Education would be designed for scale, and measured for consistency. Rao, who had spent over two decades at BITS, knew this wouldn't be easy. But he also sensed that Yasaswy was building a new model for professional education. He wanted to join that game. With that decision, the IBS flight took off.

Rao became the operational anchor and was designated Director. All nine campus coordinators reported to him. He introduced the discipline and systems he had seen at BITS. Yasaswy stayed closely involved, chairing key meetings and tracking progress. He delegated but never disengaged. 'He was hands-on from the start,' Rao said. 'Every milestone had his fingerprints on it.'

Together, they managed to do the impossible—run nine business schools like one. Rao focused on process control and team management, while Yasaswy concentrated on positioning. It was a high-trust, high-intensity working relationship. While Rao earned praise for managing the operations seamlessly, Yasaswy kept his eyes on the horizon. The two men complemented each other well, but the balance would be tested when ICFAI decided to enter engineering education.

In 2002, ICFAI Tech was announced. Yasaswy saw the technical education space as the next frontier. He believed that India's engineering graduates needed more than equations—they needed to communicate, lead, and solve real-world problems. Rao was asked to shift focus from IBS and take charge of building ICFAI Tech.

Though Rao accepted the assignment, he had reservations. IBS was now stable while ICFAI Tech still had a beating heart. The shift required a change in mindset. Engineering institutions were far more regulated. Nevertheless, Rao took on the task, and the next phase of their partnership began.

From the outset, the two differed in approach. While Rao preferred to scale ICFAI Tech at the same pace as IBS, Yasaswy, wanted to proceed cautiously. He viewed the two institutions as parts of a larger universe, each with its own growth curve.

The key point of contention soon emerged: AICTE recognition. ICFAI was legally permitted to run its programmes as a private university without AICTE approval. Yasaswy believed this autonomy was central to ICFAI's philosophy. Rao, however, faced flak. Without AICTE recognition, some ICFAI Tech graduates found qualifying for public sector jobs challenging. Recruiters raised concerns. Parents asked difficult questions.

When the problem persisted, Rao brought it to Yasaswy armed with data, student feedback, and even examples of placement rejections.

'We are seeing increasing resistance from recruiters,' Rao said. 'Some students have already lost offers. This is beginning to hurt.'

Yasaswy remained composed but resolute. 'We're a university. That status was granted by the UGC. We are not obligated to seek AICTE approval.'

Rao acknowledged the legality but persisted. 'The question is not compliance. It is perception. If we want to build trust, we have to engage the regulator to the extent that our students are not disadvantaged.'

His voice was steady, calm, and unwavering. 'It's not about rules. It's about reputation.'

The exchange stayed tense. Yasaswy was clear. 'Once you allow external control, the autonomy we value will erode. The regulator will dictate infrastructure, staffing, and pedagogy. That's not the model we are building.'

Rao understood that he had to go with it, and the conversation exposed a difference in belief systems. Their once-seamless rhythm began to thin.

Rao continued to do his job with diligence. He built faculty systems, upgraded academic processes, and introduced training programmes for the staff. But the AICTE question remained unresolved. Faculty morale fluctuated. Parents stayed anxious. Some students questioned the long-term value of their degrees.

By 2006, after over a decade of service, Rao began to feel the toll. The early momentum had slowed, and institutional fatigue had set in. It felt like time to hand over the baton.

He informed Yasaswy of his decision quietly. They met in Yasaswy's office one last time. Two men who had built institutions together were now preparing to part ways.

For a few seconds, neither spoke.

Then Yasaswy said, 'You've pushed the system forward. That has made a difference.'

Rao nodded, his voice steady. 'It's been a privilege. I came for the model. I stayed for the mission.'

Between them, too much had already been said in work, not words. Rao walked out the same way he had come years ago—measured, self-contained, and quietly proud.

Betting on Bhushan

Mumbai doesn't forgive failure.

By late 2002, ICFAI's Mumbai campus looked like one—a rented floor at Khalsa College, two classrooms, and a vanishing trick of faculty. One of the first-generation IBSs, it was already on life support.

That was when N.J. Yasaswy took a call to revive the faltering outpost. The man who answered that call was Dr Y.K. Bhushan.

After decades at NMIMS and the Bankers Training College, Bhushan was ready for quieter years. But when

Panduranga Rao spoke, Bhushan didn't need convincing. The cause was enough.

Bhushan's early days at ICFAI were not easy. In a city obsessed with pedigree, IBS was a hard sell. Bhushan had to fight for every inch. He saw what others didn't. Yasaswy's plan wasn't about rankings. He was seeking to build quality and make it accessible. Bhushan read that intent and aligned with it. That's how the Mumbai campus went from a question mark to a quiet triumph.

Yasaswy brought the clarity, and Bhushan the commitment. By 2011, the campus had grown to over eight hundred students. But the journey was not linear. Between 2009 and 2010, questions erupted around the recognition of ICFAI's programmes. Competitors fanned rumours, parents panicked, and students threatened to leave.

It was a test of leadership. Bhushan responded, drafting a point-by-point rebuttal to dispel the misinformation. He shared it across campuses, gave talks, and answered angry questions. Only a handful left. The rest stayed.

Yasaswy only intervened when it mattered.

Once, ICFAI was facing a financial crunch, and cost-cutting became imperative. At one point, even the evening tea on campus was under review.

Bhushan protested. 'Tea keeps the team together.'

Yasaswy smiled. 'Then keep it. But cut somewhere else.' That was classic Yasaswy—firm on systems, flexible on humanity.

Bhushan also pushed for greater focus on HR. 'We had strong systems,' he said, 'but we needed to look after people too.'

Enrolments rose. The faculty stayed loyal, even without the benefits of the Sixth Pay Commission. Corporate placements improved. IBS Mumbai climbed, second only to Hyderabad in student preference.

Quietly, Yasaswy had begun to rewire the model. He moved ICFAI from a hub-and-spoke structure to a more federated system, giving campus heads like Bhushan a greater voice.

He shifted the terminology, calling it 'coordinating office' instead of 'head office'.

Not that the system was perfect. Bhushan acknowledges that ICFAI could be a closed loop with limited engagement with industry. He also flagged the uniformity issue—campus heads with vastly different experience levels were treated equally. Over time, that loosened. High-performing campuses were encouraged to 'fly higher'.

There were other risks—regulatory uncertainty loomed large. Yasaswy saw this early. He spoke about acquiring campuses, diversifying courses, and preparing for possible clampdowns.

Three to four years into his tenure, Yasaswy told Bhushan, 'This is the campus we had written off—and now it's flourishing.' That single sentence, Bhushan says, was his highest compliment.

'Trust is the highest form of capital,' Yasaswy once told a colleague.

Mumbai was proof enough.

Chapter 20

The Quiet Revolutionaries

Some came to build. Others were summoned to fix. J.P. Ramappa built schools from scratch. T.R.K. Rao turned around one that was falling apart. Both walked into storms, and left behind calm.

Building Schools

The advertisement wasn't loud.

It invited IIT-IIM alumni, preferably in their fifties, with industry experience, for a leadership role in an educational institution.

At fifty-six, J.P. Ramappa's innings at Sakthi Gas had just ended. When someone suggested that he take it easy, he laughed it off. 'Not yet.'

He spotted the ICFAI ad and paused. He had heard of the institute's reputation, and more importantly, its founder's name carried weight in academic and professional circles.

Ramappa applied. His first meeting was with A.V. Vedpuriswar, nearly two decades younger. Ved wondered if someone from a complex industry could make the leap into fast-paced academia. Something in Ramappa's confidence said yes.

Ramappa was asked to meet the Big Boss.

The interview began not with a question but with a surprise. Yasaswy handed him a cup of coffee, personally brewed.

Ramappa was surprised. Leaders of his stature didn't serve coffee. But then again, Yasaswy didn't follow scripts.

'What attracts you to this place?'

Ramappa spoke of Sakthi Gas, its closure, and the quiet hunger to build something that outlasted balance sheets. Yasaswy listened, unreadable. Then, without ceremony, he placed the cup down.

'Build us a School of Information Technology,' he said. 'You have four months.'

Four months. To go from nothing to a functioning school? Crazy.

Yasaswy didn't handhold you; he handed you the challenge. He picked people like chess pieces—not for who they were, but for how they moved under pressure.

Ramappa reported for duty in December 2003. Soon, he realized that at ICFAI departments functioned like business units. Finance tracked every rupee. Admissions ran like a special-forces unit. HR, Marketing, IT, Facilities, and Career Services all had clearly defined outcomes. Ramappa said, 'It was like walking onto a factory floor.' Only this one produced institutions, leaders, and graduates.

For the first two months, he didn't sketch a syllabus. Yasaswy's instruction was explicit: 'Walk the halls. Understand the system.' So he observed. He slipped into classrooms in the morning, sipped tea with the faculty in the afternoons, and took notes in the evening.

One day, a guy from Facilities took him to 65 Nagarjuna Hills.

What he saw was four floors, bare columns, and no wall. It looked like a parking lot. This was where ISIT (ICFAI School of Information Technology) was to come up.

Ramappa stood alone on the rough floor, notepad

in hand. 'Classrooms, labs, collaborative rooms, ergonomic chairs, charging ports, natural light, fire exits.' He jotted down colours. 'Blues and greens calm the eye.' He imagined students working late, devices plugged in, and ideas bouncing off whiteboards. He thought of faculty lounges with enough elbow room.

The curriculum was next. Ramappa approached it like a chef crafting a new dish. He wanted content that mattered, tools students would use, ideas they could apply, and teachers who could teach without putting the room to sleep. In interviews, he'd ask, 'Have you taught a class where half the students didn't doze off?'

Admissions turned him into a salesman. He visited colleges, met parents, and shook hands with principals. Faculty hiring became an obsession. He wanted practitioners who could engage. The campus began to take shape—seven classrooms, breakout zones, discussion rooms, lounges, and faculty cabins. And it was delivered in the promised four months.

Ramappa recalled inviting Yasaswy to see the completed ISIT campus. They stood on the rooftop as dusk settled over Punjagutta. Yasaswy pointed at a rock near a mosque. 'Do you know why this place is called Punjagutta?'

Ramappa shook his head.

'It comes from *punjaa* and *gutta*. Paw prints on a hill. See that mark there? That's the paw.'

Ramappa looked, saw it, and smiled.

The day ISIT opened, hundred and twenty students walked through the door. Two years later, every single one was placed. But just when Ramappa thought he could breathe, Yasaswy turned the page.

At the post-launch review, Yasaswy was brief. He leaned back and said, 'Let's open in Bengaluru and Vizag.'

Ramappa blinked. 'Shouldn't we consolidate?'

'If we wait for the perfect moment,' Yasaswy replied, 'we'll miss the bus. Expansion has momentum. You go now, or you don't go at all.' That was Yasaswy's rhythm. Once something worked, he scaled it fast.

Soon, the next curveball followed: 'Let's start a School of Human Resources.'

By now, Ramappa had learnt not to flinch. He leaned on his industry background, designed a curriculum recruiters would love, and got the model running. Then came the School of Marketing Studies and, shortly after, the School of Finance!

Each school had a director. Ramappa worked behind the scenes, building systems, streamlining faculty hiring, aligning placements, and reporting to the man who had lit the fire.

The blaze was spreading—that is until 2008 hit like a storm.

The timing could not have been worse. A court questioned the legitimacy of ICFAI Tech's degree. Students and their parents were worried.

In one of the meetings, ideas flew. Most of them were band-aid solutions.

Finally, Yasaswy stood up. 'We'll offer students two choices,' he said. 'Stay with us—we'll guarantee education and placement. Or leave—and we refund every rupee.'

Someone boldly asked, 'But Sir, what about the financial loss?'

'What's the price of integrity?'

Around ninety students opted to leave. The rest stayed—and graduated with jobs.

Between 2008 and 2011, Ramappa held ISIT steady through its roughest phase. However, the vagaries of the market including the impending court cases, possible cannibalization, etc. forced Yasaswy to pull down the schools.

'It hurt,' Ramappa said later. 'It felt like a part of me was being shuttered.'

Faculty members, administrators, and support staff were either redeployed within ICFAI or compensated generously.

Yasaswy spoke to Ramappa. 'Ideas have lives,' he said. 'When they're done, don't mourn. Celebrate, and move on.'

That was Yasaswy—surgical, not sentimental.

Yasaswy didn't build empires—he built institution builders. He lit fires, then stepped back to watch them burn bright.

The Turnaround Man

The first meeting was a washout.

It was April 2004. T.R.K. Rao, Chief General Manager of NABARD, had come to Hyderabad, looking to start his second innings. A friend nudged him toward Yasaswy, saying, 'He's building something that'll outlive him. You could help.'

Rao walked into ICFAI Headquarters, riding on thirty-plus years of institutional experience. Yasaswy asked, almost casually, 'Will you teach?'

The banker blinked. 'I'm not here for a classroom role, Sir. I'm looking at something strategic.'

'I see. I don't know the connection, then.'

Rao stood up, smiled, and thanked him for his time. 'He has his profile. I have mine,' he told himself.

Two days later, a call came. Rao was in Chennai. 'Sir, can you reroute your ticket?' It was Vedpuriswar. 'Boss would like to meet.'

The second meeting didn't last five minutes. Yasaswy just handed over an envelope. Inside it was an offer letter—signed, sealed and ready.

Rao looked up. 'I'll serve my notice at NABARD.' Yasaswy just nodded. As if it was already done.

On 29 September 2004, Rao reported for duty.

'There are no departments yet,' Yasaswy said. Spend some

time with Ved. Visit our several units. Watch them function. Then we'll decide.'

Rao sat in classrooms, listened to faculty discussions, and observed decisions. A regulator by training, he expected red tape. Instead, he found an institution with the scale of a university and the speed of a start-up.

He was being considered for press and publications when the storm hit.

The ICFAI School of Marketing Studies (ISMS) was in a free fall. A bunch of disillusioned students and a director who'd quietly exited meant they were in a deep hole. Yasaswy called Rao to fix it. 'I'm giving you a broken school. You're free to say no.'

'What's my latitude?' Rao asked.

'You will report to me. There are no gatekeepers. Take the decisions you need to. You don't have to circle with me every time. If you fail, I'll take the rap. If you succeed, the credit is yours.'

Of course, he didn't say this in those exact same words but that was the essence. The operative phrase was 'I trust you.'

Rao nodded. 'Then I'll take it.'

The next morning, he walked into ISMS.

The classroom air was thick with distrust. Sharp, vocal, tired students sat with folded arms and cold stares. Rao started with a schedule.

'From today,' he announced, 'classes run from 7 to 11 a.m., and again from 4 to 8 p.m. Afternoons are for self-study, rest, or internships.'

He brought in IGNOU audio lectures and gave students headsets. He also hired Dr T.N. Rao, a former RAW strategist who turned war case studies into marketing simulations.

For placements, he called people he knew from his earlier life—people now in senior slots at ITC, Asian Paints, and

Hindustan Unilever. That's how all twenty students under his wing got placed. Coca-Cola showed up on Day Zero. ICFAI's black sheep had become its crown jewel.

Yasaswy called a review. At the end of it, he asked, 'Rao Garu, have you filed the incentive forms for your team?'

'Incentive? Didn't know there was one.'

Yasaswy smiled faintly. 'Colonel Prasad will give you the format. Submit it.' Rao was halfway to the door when Yasaswy added, 'Include your name too.'

That was leadership without a lecture—a quiet insistence that success deserves to be seen, even at the top.

In 2008, when all the four focused schools were shut down, Rao moved to corporate communications.

ICFAI was under attack. *The Times of India* had run a damaging story. Yasaswy didn't rage. He called Rao.

Rao tapped his old network—his uncle had once led the Indian Federation of Working Journalists—and met Kingshuk Nag, the editor.

Yasaswy hosted Nag and his wife for dinner at Grand Kakatiya. It was just straight talk about what ICFAI had built and why it mattered. The coverage softened. The rumours dried up.

By now, Rao had also become Yasaswy's legal sounding board.

Distance learning and the INC had triggered legal landmines. Rao suggested that they engage top-tier legal firms. That's how Luthra and Luthra came in. Soon, ICFAI had briefings from Mukul Rohatgi, Arun Jaitley, and Rohinton Nariman.

Today, Rao is the Chancellor of ICFAI University, Jharkhand. When asked what ICFAI needs most, he doesn't hesitate. 'A bottom-up inclusive vision.'

And of Yasaswy, he said, 'He gave me a ladder. And stood back and watched me climb.'

Chapter 21

Consultant's Code

When the market froze, Yasaswy didn't pause to complain. He rolled up his sleeves and built. March and Cygnus weren't passion projects—they were lifelines. One gave stranded MBAs a way forward. The other taught them how to think.

A Missed Train

March began as a lifeboat.

In 2003, the economy stalled, and MBA placements flattened. ICFAI had two thousand students graduating. No company was hiring, and no one knew how long the drought would last. That's when Yasaswy made one of his wildest moves—he conjured two companies almost overnight: He didn't wait for demand; he created it. March for market research and Cygnus for corporate publishing. He hired a hundred students, put them on payroll, and threw them into action.

By the time Sridhar Chari walked into Yasaswy's office a few months later, the storm had passed, but the tent was still up.

'I'm back in Hyderabad,' Chari said. 'Bombay's done.' He had known Yasaswy from his Nagarjuna days.

'Join us.'

'What's the mandate?'

'I don't know yet. But I hire for a long-term fit—not for roles.'

It wasn't a random hire. Chari had spent over a decade with Nagarjuna, where Yasaswy had been a sounding board to its patriarch, K.V.K. Raju. At ICFAI, Chari eased into the publications division, reading case studies, writing reports, and waiting for clarity.

That clarity arrived soon.

'The man heading March is leaving,' Yasaswy said one morning. 'Can you take over?'

March felt like a leftover from a firefight—thirty employees, a few scattered clients, and no clear model. Within months, Chari turned the wreck into a research engine. They handled airport surveys for Sony, site feasibility reports for INC campuses, and consumer studies that went deep into cities, villages, and habits.

Soon, March began bidding for QCBS tenders and competing against Nielsen and PwC. By 2005, it had grown into a full-fledged research outfit with eighty analysts.

It serviced ministries, state departments, and global institutions. Clients included the World Bank, Aga Khan Foundation, HPCL, Indian Oil, Tata Teleservices, and DuPont. March became a trusted name in satisfaction indices, market forecasts, feasibility studies, and consumer pulse checks.

Chari still remembers the day Yasaswy sat through a review meeting and quietly said, 'I've never seen a better review from March in this room.'

It wasn't loud. It didn't need to be. When Yasaswy praised, it was a verdict.

Even as March scaled, Yasaswy had another fire to fight. The CFA Institute in the US had filed a trademark case against ICFAI, challenging its use of the CFA designation.

'I want you to join a two-man team,' Yasaswy told Chari. 'We're going to fight this in the US.'

The law bills were staggering, but Yasaswy was ready to spend crores defending an Indian qualification.

Chari attended hearings, sat through depositions, and trained as a mediator. The case stretched on, then ended. ICFAI lost. Yasaswy accepted the verdict, and withdrew the CFA tag.

But the fight had unlocked a larger ambition; a global itch.

'There's an Indian diaspora out there,' Yasaswy said. 'They want MBAs for their children—degrees with context, not just cost.'

He asked Chari to launch Indian-style MBA programmes in Mauritius, New Zealand, Germany, and the UK. Chari travelled, held meetings with Boards, assessed real estate, and tested regulatory waters. For a while, it seemed ICFAI might go global.

Then came 2008. Regulators tightened. Funding dried up. March, again, stood at the edge.

By now, March was handling projects for the Ministry of Tourism, the Airports Authority of India, and various state departments. In the private sector, they serviced nearly every telecom player and worked with Reliance Retail and Dr. Reddy's.

At one point, March floated a strategy to grow via mergers and acquisitions—targeting three smaller agencies to expand into knowledge process outsourcing. But regulators were tightening the noose. Education entities were expected to stay within their lane. Cash was tight. The M&A plan didn't fly.

In 2009, ICFAI decided to exit the consulting space and refocus on education.

Two IBS alumni working at March, Arvind Singh (IBS Gurgaon) and Amarnath Rapaka (IBS Hyderabad), approached Chari. 'Can we take over March? Will you mentor us?'

Chari sounded Yasaswy and the latter agreed to the transfer. March was handed over and Sapience Research was born.

Chari stayed on to guide them. Today, Arvind runs the firm with fifteen full-time staff and clients across India. Chari continues as their mentor.

But behind this business thriller lies a more personal arc—a friendship that never quite bloomed—not for lack of warmth but because of too much reverence.

Between meetings and market studies, Chari and Yasaswy spoke often—of poetry, Wordsworth, Tennyson, and Ghalib. They shared a love for literature, for rhythm, and for lines that stayed.

One day, Yasaswy said, 'Let's go to the Midlands. Take our wives. Read Wordsworth where he wrote. Walk the woods he walked.'

Tickets were booked.

Then, Chari's mother fell critically ill. He cancelled. Yasaswy didn't flinch. 'I'll cancel mine too. We'll go another time.'

That time never came.

'Perhaps I should've rescheduled,' Chari would later say. 'But I didn't. I was too much in awe. That's my regret.'

He paused. 'We could've been true friends, but I held back.' And then, he added softly, 'He never built walls. But he never invited you in either. And I never crossed that invisible line.'

When ICFAI began downsizing in 2010, Chari stepped away voluntarily.

In five years, he had worn three hats. And seen three sides of the same man.

- The Boss: Exacting, brilliant, and brutally honest
- The Institution Builder: Visionary, fearless, always ahead
- The Unfulfilled Friend: So brilliant, even friends held back from knocking

'He could've been a great friend,' Chari said. 'He certainly was a great leader.'

If March was a test of speed, Cygnus would become a test of depth.

Think Tank

O.R.S. Rao wasn't looking for a job. After decades in the Indian industry—BHEL, HCL, GMR—he had earned his right to live in peace!

Then came a call that didn't feel like a pitch. 'We're not hiring,' the voice said. 'We're building.' It was Yasaswy.

They met in a quiet conference room.

'We've built classrooms,' Yasaswy said. 'Now, let's build a think tank. Not just for our students. For India.' Then, after a pause, 'Rao Garu, I want it to become our brain trust. Can you lead it?'

That day, Cygnus Business Consulting and Research was born.

Yasaswy called it 'knowledge beyond curriculum'. Rao called it 'a godsent opportunity'.

And just like that, Rao, the engineer-executive, became a consultant and later an educator. If Yasaswy was the architect, Rao was the structural engineer—quiet, precise, and willing to get his hands dirty.

In weeks, a modest building lit up. Laptops hummed. Analyst calls filled the air. Reports flew out—monthly bulletins, deep dives, and company profiles. Two thousand five hundred firms were analysed. Working capital cycles, forex exposures, boardroom reshuffles—nothing was off-limits.

Over five thousand students were trained. Clients paid for feasibility studies, portfolios, and market entries. Among them were Aditya Birla, Godrej, ONGC, Infosys, HSBC, Adobe, TCS and ICICI. Consulates, global banks, and trade missions also joined its clientele, which included more than eight hundred organizations—from multinationals to PSUs.

Cygnus changed the culture internally. The faculty began citing Cygnus data in classrooms, and portals like *CKP* and *i3* became reference points.

Yasaswy pushed for branches in Delhi, Mumbai, Bengaluru and Kolkata. To serve global clients, he planted a flag in London.

Behind it all, Rao moved relentlessly. Under him, monthly bulletins went out, tracking the Indian economy, decoding global movements, and diving deep into sectors.

By 2011, Cygnus was ICFAI's sharpest credibility engine.

For Yasaswy, it proved that education could be weaponized—applied, monetized and globalized. For Rao, it proved that the quietest bets can change the texture of an institution.

He hadn't come looking for a job. He came by chance—and stayed to build a legacy.

PART VI

The Man

Character is how you treat those who can do nothing for you.

—JOHANN VON GOETHE (COMMONLY ATTRIBUTED)

Chapter 22

The Man Who Walked You to the Door

1984

It's a week since the assassination of Prime Minister. Indira Gandhi.

At the Yasaswy household, the dinner table is set. A seven-year-old Tejaswy poses a question.

'Nanna, how can there be a god who can control the whole world?' He had just learnt that there were billions of people on earth. It seemed like far too many for one god to manage.

Yasaswy looked at his son and smiled. 'Do you think it's not possible?'.

The boy paused. 'Even my teacher struggles to manage twenty kids in class. How can someone manage everyone in the world?'

'Maybe it is a challenging task,' Yasaswy said, passing the dal.

That was Yasaswy's way. He never shut down questions. He widened them. But before we narrate more about Tejaswy, let's talk about a friendship.

A Lifelong Bond

Normally, by six, the noise around N.J. Yasaswy would dissolve. Like Cinderella after the ball, he would transform.

For the next hour, it was just the two of them—he and Sobharani Nandury, his wife.

They walked through KBR Park every evening, a ritual they rarely missed. They talked about everything—from the day's challenges at ICFAI to the feel of the breeze.

At home, dinner was family time when the four would gather together. Yasaswy, Shobarani, Tejaswy and Vennela.

Food was never carried to the bedroom, and television didn't compete for attention. Conversations were freewheeling; school gossip, national politics, ethical dilemmas and odd jokes.

Sobharani didn't work at ICFAI, but she was not a bystander either.

She knew the headlines, footnotes, and fine print. She remembered the day Alfred C. Morley first met Yasaswy. She remembered when Morley came home.

When she couldn't travel with him, Yasaswy sent letters, each one a window into his journey. They spoke of meals shared, strangers met, landscapes admired, and quiet vows: 'We'll return here someday together.' And true to his word, he did.

Their home was forever open for friends and colleagues.

It all began with a schoolgirl's wish.

In 1972, a few months after the Indo-Pak War, a teenaged Sobharani told her father, 'I want to marry only someone highly educated.' It was her way of stalling a possible early marriage.

A little under two years later, her father returned with a young man from Tenali—N.J. Yasaswy.

They married in Ongole on 5 December 1973. She had once dreamed of studying at Santiniketan, but that dream evaporated. In its place, they built mutual respect and the pure joy of each other's company.

Their son Tejaswy was born in 1977, the year India voted out the Congress for the first time. Their daughter Vennela arrived in 1979, as the Second Oil Crisis broke out.

By then, Yasaswy was a rising star. But at home, he was an involved father. Their children grew up amidst books, conversations, and questions that didn't always have answers.

Some moments revealed Yasaswy's core. In 1990, when Sobharani suffered a fall and injured her face, the doctor at Apollo listed three plastic surgeons. One of them was the best, and the most expensive.

Yasaswy didn't hesitate. 'We'll go to the best.'

The surgery was successful, but the doctor refused the fee.

'I'm from Guntur,' he said. 'Your husband was our hero in our growing-up years.'

Sobharani felt a quiet pride. Yasaswy later donated that money in the surgeon's name to the Republic School. It was his way of saying 'thank you.'

Through all this, he read obsessively—Shakespeare, Vedanta, finance. He could absorb anything, explain it simply, and move on. Music, to him, was humanity in another language.

He adored his parents, and his mother remained his emotional anchor. 'I saw her in him,' Sobharani once said, 'and I saw him in her.'

To the world, he was a visionary who built institutions. To Sobharani, he remained the boy from Tenali—the one who didn't let ambition overshadow their bond.

The First Classroom

Back to the seven-year-old and his questions.

A few months after the god debate, Tejaswy came home from school with another strong view. 'They should ban drugs,' he declared.

Yasaswy disagreed. 'Drugs are bad. But banning them isn't the answer.'

'What? You want them to be legal?'

Yasaswy didn't raise his voice. He said, 'You see when you ban something, it doesn't disappear. People just find other ways of getting it—like students sneaking cigarettes behind buildings.' He paused. 'Once it's banned, it becomes a crime. Crime brings fear, black markets, and police. That's more dangerous than the drug.'

He looked up, thoughtful. 'What if, instead of banning, the government taxed drugs heavily and used that money to educate people?'

Tejaswy voiced this argument at school, much to his teacher's dismay.

One day, Yasaswy said, 'We shouldn't have asked the British to leave India. We should've colonized them.'

'What do you mean?' asked Tejaswy.

'Well, if we had stayed British citizens, we could have moved to England—millions of us. We would have become the majority and could have taken over the empire from inside.'

One may never know whether he was serious or not. But one thing was clear—Yasaswy never wanted his son to take the world at face value.

Before Tejaswy turned ten, his father gave him George Orwell's *Animal Farm* (1945). They discussed it, especially the line: 'Some pigs are more equal than others.'

Then came Orwell's *1984* (1949), M.K. Gandhi's *My*

Experiments with Truth (1929), Shakespeare, and the Bhagavad Gita. Each book led to evening talks and sharp debates.

As the boy grew older, the books became about business leaders—John Sculley from Pepsi and Apple, Thomas Watson Jr. from IBM, and political leaders such as Nelson Mandela.

Yasaswy never said, 'Be like this man.' He asked, 'What did you learn from his journey?' Even when his son made choices he didn't fully agree with, Yasaswy never stood in the way.

By the time Tejaswy left for college, he had received two educations—one from school and one from a man who never taught with answers.

At dinner he'd begin: 'Did you know that the word "Czar" comes from Caesar?'

He'd then link Roman history and Russian diplomacy, throw in a quiz mid-sentence, and expect everyone to answer. 'When you disagreed or dared to correct him,' says his daughter Vennela Nandury, 'he didn't get upset. He listened, countered if he could—and if not, he changed the topic!' He loved being right but not more than he loved being curious.

To the world, Yasaswy was a towering intellect. To his children, he was just Nanna Garu—often found surrounded by books, notes and pads.

'He was always writing,' Vennela recalls. 'Reading. Thinking aloud. That's the image I carry.'

But there was another side to this cerebral man: a sense of humour.

Anyone who walked into their home was fair game. Yasaswy would invent quizzes on the spot that were elaborate puzzles with traps. Most didn't realize they'd walked into one until it was too late.

Except once.

'One of my cousins, Aishwarya, Sankara Garu's daughter, outsmarted him,' Vennela grins. 'It was a quiz on family relationships. Who's whose uncle if this person is married to that person's niece...etc. She cracked it. And he was stunned.'

At home, he wasn't exactly a disciplinarian. He was precise, yes. Punctual, definitely. And his anger was forgotten in an instant.

When it came to money, the kids were never put on allowances. Not out of frugality but philosophy.

'Money is available for what you need,' he'd say. No fixed pocket money. No weekly budgets. Open access, built on trust and need.

Books were sacred. No amount was too high, and no subject was too obscure. He never said no and encouraged her to ask for more. It was his way of planting a lifelong love for learning.

Vennela completed her schooling in Hyderabad and later pursued her Master's in England.

Among Yasaswy's lesser-known dreams was the Republic School.

'He used to joke about it when we were young,' she says. 'He'd say education should be free. We'll only charge for the air the students breathe.'

The joke became a vision. With Vennela's experience in The Art of Living's children's programmes, and a vacant building in Fateh Nagar, the first Republic School came up. 'In his usual style, one was never enough,' she laughs. Funded entirely by Yasaswy, it scaled to ten full-fledged schools and over twenty-five 'one-room' set-ups, reaching nearly five thousand children.

And then around 2012, it paused.

Sustaining the model without a corpus was proving difficult. Other philanthropic trusts stepped in, including one

led by former Infosys Chairman Dr G.K. Jayaram, ensuring the schools continued under different banners.

'It didn't feel like a closure,' Vennela says. 'It felt like a relay. We passed the baton.'

For all his public stature, Yasaswy was a private man. He had no hobbies beyond reading and no social life outside of his family and work. A minimalist, his life revolved around his home, his office, and his bookshelf. If he wasn't working, he was home. And if he was home, he was reading. Or laughing.

He wasn't extroverted, but when he was in the company of people, his wit lit up the space.'

He made it clear early on: ICFAI was never going to be a family fiefdom. 'We respected that,' says Vennela. 'He wanted it to be professional. Built to last. Not inherited.'

Still, didn't she ever want to run it? Didn't she feel the tug of legacy?

'No,' she says. 'It was never about ownership. For him, it was about contribution.'

Both Tejaswy and she were involved in different ways. But the expectation to lead never existed. Yasaswy had built ICFAI to be bigger than any individual. His children were free to pursue their own paths.

For Vennela, that path was The Art of Living. 'It was a personal choice,' she says. 'Not a rejection of his work, but a reflection of my own calling.'

❧

Yasaswy's didn't just speak of values. He lived by them—in meeting rooms, at dining tables, and during the quiet moments that revealed his character.

When Hyderabad moved to sedans, Yasaswy stayed with his good old Ambassador '8558'. Friends pleaded with him. 'Upgrade.'

For years, he smiled and declined. It wasn't about money. 'What does a car do? Takes you from Point A to B. My Amby still does that job,' he'd say.

Finally, in 2004, he agreed.

One day in Kolkata, he stood up to speak. The microphone failed.

Technicians rushed, but Yasaswy continued, unbothered. Twenty minutes later, the mike was working again but no one noticed.

They were already listening, hooked to his oration.

J. Nrupender Rao, Executive Chairman of Pennar Industries, called Yasaswy 'a lifeline'. Yasaswy helped during Pennar's restructuring in the late 1990s. At a critical meeting with Penrillian, their UK partner, he dissected financials and laid out a future so compelling that the British board rose to give him a standing ovation.

Neeraja Vangala, T.S.R.K. Lohit's daughter recalled the vibrant dynamic between Yasaswy and his mother—a clash of unwavering wills. They exchanged playful barbs and teased each other relentlessly. He dismissed her views as outdated. She retorted, 'You're far too modern to be taken seriously.'

But underneath all that was a mutual respect that had lasted a lifetime.

His lunch was simple—dal, rice and vegetable. But what stood out wasn't what was on the plate. When a guest visited them, and after the meal was served, Yasaswy quietly stood up, carried his own plate to the sink, washed, and wiped it dry. There was no fanfare, no maid summoned, just a gesture that said, 'Everyone pulls their weight.'

You'd expect that from your grandfather, not from the founder of a major university.

In Board meetings the feedback was sharp. Praise was rare, and so when it came, it was gold. After meetings, every single time, no matter how brief the visit, Yasaswy would rise and walk you to the door.

When Bhushan turned seventy-five, a quiet celebration was planned in Mumbai. Just close friends and family. Many assumed Yasaswy wouldn't make it, but he arrived accompanied by S.K. Sharma, Director of IBS Hyderabad. He chatted with Bhushan's grandchildren, asked them about their dreams, and left them starstruck.

Philosopher Abroad

Dr C.M. Prasad, who had left India in 1968 for a career in psychiatry in the US, reunited with Yasaswy in 2010.

In the in-between years he had watched his friend rise to superstardom. But when Yasaswy arrived that day with a suitcase and a smile, it felt like 1964 again.

During the weekend they mimicked Telugu accents, poked fun at teachers with strange nicknames, argued about who was worse at geometry, and drank filter coffee. It was déjà vu.

'Success didn't change him,' said Prasad. 'It deepened what was already there.'

'He wore the hat of a childhood friend that weekend,' Prasad said. 'Just two boys from Guntur, catching up across a lifetime.' They promised to meet again. Destiny, however, had other plans.

A day later, in Chicago, he was a guest again—this time at the home of Rajeshwar Rao, a soft-spoken CEO based in Indiana. His wife had insisted they host her old friend, Sobharani, and her husband. Rajeshwar had agreed reluctantly. He wasn't sure what to expect.

It began over tea in Columbus—casual, almost perfunctory. But by the next evening, the conversation had deepened. Sitting cross-legged in a quiet corner of a temple, Yasaswy traced the arc of Hinduism from the oral Rig Veda to its colonial distortions and into its modern-day meaning. Rajeshwar sat, spellbound.

'It was like talking to a monk who read *The Wall Street Journal*,' he later said. 'He knew how to connect ideas across time, space, and economics.'

At that moment, Rajeshwar remembered a line from Oliver Goldsmith about the village schoolmaster and how '… that one small head could carry all he knew.' But now, it wasn't the village schoolmaster. It was the schoolmaster's son.

When the visit ended, they shook hands and promised to meet again soon.

And pray, what has been the greatest proof of his powerful legacy? That the man who never put himself first is remembered first. Always.

Long before he built campuses, he built a certain calm. Sometimes impact wasn't in what he said—it was in what he chose not to say.

Chapter 23

Silence That Spoke

Some men make a splash for the moment. Others create a ripple that lasts forever. N.J. Yasaswy belonged to the latter kind. His presence was easy to miss in a crowded room—until he spoke. And then he owned it.

He didn't wear success on his sleeve. He wore it like his shirt—simple, quiet and perfectly ironed.

Abburi Chaya Devi recognized his presence instantly. At one event, he stated with quiet conviction, 'If education does not uplift the most disadvantaged, it has failed its purpose.' The remark was not dramatic; it was deliberate. It echoed like a distant bell. 'He was a reformer without the clamour,' she said later.

But the story hadn't begun on a stage. It began with an answer sheet.

In the 1960s, Parimi Anjaneya Sharma, an English teacher with a red pen and a pile of coded scripts, paused at one that stood out. The handwriting was neat, the grammar flawless, and the thinking mature. Curious, Sharma traced the code, and got the name—Yasaswy.

Years later, when that boy became the man behind India's most ambitious education model, Sharma wasn't surprised. What he had seen in that answer sheet—order, clarity and restraint—one day defined the institutions Yasaswy would build.

Few people knew how deeply he cared about culture. Even as he imported cases from Harvard, he quietly funded Telugu learning kits. Where many saw small towns as low-priority, he saw them as India's unclaimed promise. 'Education,' he once said, 'must not just be smart. It must feel like home.'

At home, he was no different. Sobharani never saw *the founder*. He didn't scold. He nudged. 'He could make a single raised eyebrow feel like a courtroom argument,' she laughed. Even disagreement came gently, often coated with humour.

When Tejaswy once asked, 'Why don't you ever raise your voice?' Yasaswy smiled and said, 'Because if I shout, I can't hear myself think.'

He had his quirks. He hated waste. Avoided shopping. Wore the same few shirts in rotation until someone forcibly replaced them. Gadgets delighted him like toys. And he carried that minimalism everywhere.

Sri Ramana, a journalist who met him in 1985, remembered the day Yasaswy showed up at a newsroom.

No pitch deck. No entourage. Just an idea: India needed financial literacy that didn't stop at the boardroom but reached the street vendor, the housewife, the student. 'He didn't come to impress,' Ramana wrote. 'He came to recruit our conscience.'

His decisiveness set him apart—not reckless, but guided by an unshakable clarity 'Speed is fine,' he once remarked, 'but direction is what matters.'

He was, in many ways, a paradox in Indian public life. In a country where volume often masquerades as leadership, Yasaswy proved that power didn't need a microphone. That you could build an empire without becoming its emperor.

And so, he built. He built quietly, so that others could speak loudly. He lit lamps, but never stood beside them. When the applause came, he was already away, planning the next chapter of ICFAI.

Chapter 24

Architect of Possibility

There's a photograph in the ICFAI archives that tells you more than any press release ever could.

A man in a blue shirt walks unhurried along a Goan beach, his sleeves rolled up. Walking beside him is a younger colleague, trying to keep pace with both his steps and his thoughts. The older man is mid-sentence, talking about a book.

He's speaking of Gurcharan Das's *The Difficulty of Being Good* (2009). Can dharma survive in the modern world? What does goodness cost? How do you lead with values when the system rewards shortcuts?

The tide of the conversation rolls on. The younger man says little. He's listening, absorbing, storing away the moment. The teacher, the philosopher, the builder—whatever you called him—was doing what he always did. Asking questions that mattered.

Of course, the man is N.J. Yasaswy. A teacher at heart, wrapped in an entrepreneur's skin, he could turn a walk into a masterclass.

The problem with Indian education, he'd argue, wasn't just quality. It was the brutal unevenness of access. In cities, students were spoilt for choice. In smaller towns, they were expected to settle for mediocrity. That imbalance, to him, was a moral failure.

So, he didn't wait for policy. He built. One campus after another, each with intent. From Dehradun to Bhubaneswar, Mizoram to Jaipur, ICFAI became a relay of hope—quiet buildings in quiet places that told bright young Indians, 'You belong here too.'

But for Yasaswy, scale never meant sameness. He refused to create clones. He wanted thinkers. He wanted classrooms to feel like conversations, not control rooms.

He was sceptical of rote perfection. 'Don't tell me the answer,' he once said during a curriculum review. 'Tell me why the question matters.'

That's why he championed the case method. A case study didn't hand out moral judgements. It made you take a position. It made you defend it. It made you realize that real life doesn't come with model answers.

He ran his institutions with an entrepreneur's pace and an auditor's conscience. The numbers had to add up, but the heart had to stay intact.

His meetings often began with sharp questions—costs, conversion rates, faculty hours—but they rarely ended with just data. He'd always circle back to a simple challenge: 'What will the student feel when they step in?'

He didn't want to win on price. He tried to win on trust. Governance wasn't a subject for him. It was the instinct. People often mistook his precision for coldness.

When a marketing idea crossed a line or when someone suggested bending a rule to push admissions, he wouldn't raise his voice. He would simply ask, 'Will these still make us proud a decade from now?'

He believed that institutions must run with the lights on. 'Even a small lie,' he once said, 'sets off a vibration. And that vibration can't be controlled.'

He was not against profit. ICFAI generated a surplus—

that was no secret. But every rupee was reinvested in better infrastructure, better faculty, and better systems. He refused to take dividends, resisted vanity, and treated surplus as trust.

Self-reliance was his creed. No donations. No waiting for grants. No lobbying. If a model didn't sustain itself, it didn't deserve to live. He was obsessed with cost control—not from stinginess, but from discipline.

To him, students were not 'customers' in the transactional sense. They were *trustees* of the institution's mission.

Within ICFAI, he delegated but never disengaged. He encouraged experiments and even applauded failure, but he demanded that every failure be understood.

Even when the institution grew too large for him to touch every process, he kept a pulse on it—not through surveillance, but through systems, people and questions.

He believed that when the culture is right, control becomes unnecessary. He was not just a builder of campuses, but the architect of possibility.

The photograph from Goa remains—its edges softened by time.

In 1976, the University of Singapore—now the National University of Singapore—was looking to strengthen its accountancy department. Bhanoji Rao, a senior faculty member from the university, on leave in India, was asked to interview a prospective candidate in Hyderabad.

Even in that brief interaction, the candidate's clarity of thought, intellectual precision and calm presence left a deep impression on the interviewer. Soon, the university issued an appointment letter for the post of lecturer.

Months later, when the Singapore-based professor returned

to his office, an airmail envelope awaited him. Inside was a letter from N.J. Yasaswy. It said: 'I received the appointment letter from the University. But I am not accepting the job. I believe I have a mission to accomplish in my own country.'

In the view of the professor who first met him in 1976, his accomplishments were 'beyond anyone's imagination…the kind that make Mother India proud.'

PART VII

Final Days

When the music is over, the memory lingers.

—UNKNOWN

Chapter 25

When the Clock Stopped

12 September 2011

Just past noon, N.J. Yasaswy stood up from his chair.

'I need to go,' he said, excusing himself from the meeting he was chairing. He offered no explanation.

He told Dr Mahender J. Reddy to reschedule the Case Centre meeting for the next day. That meeting never happened.

The fever he had shrugged off with a pill had become unbearable. He walked down the steps of his office at 19 Nagarjuna Hills and got into his car. 'Apollo,' he told the driver.

It was the same hospital where he once sat on the Board. There was no urgency in his voice. Just another quiet instruction.

At Apollo, doctors ran tests. 'Viral infection,' they said. 'He'll be home soon.' Sobharani passed on the update to her mother-in-law. A few days later, the tone changed. 'Haemorrhage,' they said. 'We must operate immediately.'

8 October 2011

The day came without warning.

Tejaswy had flown in from Mumbai. Vennela sat silently by her mother. Yasaswy was wheeled into surgery, surrounded by some of the finest medical hands in the country.

He had now been in hospital for almost a month. They had expected him to be discharged that day. But a sudden cerebral haemorrhage changed everything. A few hours later, the surgeons came out. 'He didn't make it,' they said. The final diagnosis was tubercular meningitis.

The Titan was gone. There was no last lecture, no final sign-off, just a date: 8 October 2011. He was sixty-one, to turn sixty-two next February.

He had once told a journalist: 'Every day is a new, exciting day. So much can be done. Alas, time is a finite commodity.' And to someone else: 'The day I feel I can't deliver, I won't sit in this chair even for a minute.'

He had expected to be guiding until he was seventy. It's anyone's guess what ICFAI might have become with him over the last fifteen years.

Perhaps he ran too hot. Eleven universities, nine business schools, seven engineering colleges, nine law schools, a hundred and seventy-plus National Colleges, and a string of ventures—Cygnus, Magnus, March, Republic School. Even to list them is exhausting.

Then, there were the myriad legal cases cutting across the country and continents. The litigations too must have taken their toll. And finally, the loneliness of being the one everyone looked up to. The one with no real 3 a.m. friends.

Across ICFAI's campuses, disbelief hung in the air like thick fog. Nobody knew what tomorrow would look like.

Old-timers still remember where they were when the news came.

In Raipur, a Board meeting was being held. 'Boss is no more,' someone whispered. The Chancellor stood up. 'This meeting cannot go on.' A senior officer wept like a son who had lost his father.

V. P. Joy was in Mumbai. He caught the next flight, landed

in Hyderabad before sunrise, and walked straight into the house. And then, for the first and only time, he did something he'd never done when the man was alive.

He touched his feet.

'Respect,' he said later, 'isn't conditional. It's owed.'

Over two thousand five hundred people gathered at the man's Jubilee Hills residence—a professor he had coaxed out of retirement; a businessman whose sinking venture he had revived, and many more.

And in one quiet corner, his mother, Seetharamamma, now in her eighties, sat by her son's body. She rocked him gently as if she could coax the universe into giving him back.

Elsewhere, M.P. Sinha of GHRDC stopped his car on Sion Road in Mumbai and observed two minutes of silence.

Even in those final hours, Yasaswy's influence lingered. Before he left for Apollo, he had asked two senior leaders to meet a former Karnataka home minister about a campus property.

There was no push, no pressure. The minister said, 'I cannot say no to Yasaswy.' The deal closed without fuss.

Grief came later. What remained immediate and vivid were the stories.

Like the time he aged overnight while visiting his daughter in London. When people commented about it, he introduced his wife—unchanged and radiant —as his 'second wife'. It was delivered with such perfect timing that people believed him!

Within forty-eight hours of his passing away, Tejaswy Nandury stepped in as CEO. He was thirty-four.

He began with consolidation and restructured the organization. He steadied the ship, bringing peace and solace to the organization. Six months later, Tejaswy, a Stanford graduate, moved to the capital markets. Vennela found her path in service with The Art of Living Foundation.

When Tejaswy stepped back, the mantle quietly passed to two insiders. E.N. Murthy, Controller of Examinations, and V.R. Sankara, the one who rushed to N.J. Yasaswy when he saw him in a bookstore. Like the quiet leaders James C. Collins writes about in *Good to Great: Why Some Companies Make the Leap...and Others Don't* (2001), Sankara wasn't flashy but steady. And that's what the institution needed in the aftermath of the storm.

Yasaswy could've helmed a Fortune 500 company. With his razor-sharp mind, he could've been a superstar. But he chose education, where victories are slow and legacies show up years later.

Many say he deserved a Padma award. Perhaps he did. But his real reward lies elsewhere—in every student who dared to dream bigger because of him. How did he do it?

Those who knew him didn't need to ask. They had seen it in how—

- He refused to accept the world as it is.
- He never waited for permission to build.
- He walked beside his wife in KBR Park each evening.
- He argued with his son—not for dominance, but for truth.
- He remembered names, people, and details.
- He read documents like scriptures.
- He made peace with never choosing the easy path.
- He showed up. Always.

They say you can measure a man by what he builds. But with Yasaswy, the measure is how long it endures—even after the clock has stopped. Eight hundred years more—just as he had envisioned? Time will tell.

'They say time heals,' Vennela reflects. 'But with him, it's not about healing. It's about remembering—how one man could be so brilliant, so funny, so fiercely honest, and yet so tender.' A modern version of Oliver Goldsmith's description of the village schoolmaster.

Rabindranath Tagore once wrote, 'Death is not extinguishing the light; it is only putting out the lamp because the dawn has come.'

And for Yasaswy, that dawn had indeed arrived.

Chapter 26

The Roads They Took

2025

The heart of ICFAI still beats at Nagarjuna Hills, Hyderabad.

Today, ICFAI is a multi-university juggernaut.

Each year, thousands of students walk through these gates. Most never hear the full story of the man behind the name. To them, he is a framed photo on a wall. A distant legend.

But remembering Yasaswy isn't an act of nostalgia. It's a call to imagine what one life—lived with clarity and courage—can create.

Sobharani Nandury now chairs the ICFAI Society, under whose umbrella the entire network continues to grow.

V.R. Sankara leads it as President, quietly carrying forward the mission.

Many who stood by Yasaswy in those daring early years have moved on.

Dr Besant C. Raj, the anchor of ICFAI's early credibility, passed away in 2018.

Dr Prasanna Chandra, who laid the academic foundation, still teaches and mentors from his Centre for Financial Management.

M.V. Siva Ram, co-architect of the university model, now advises other institutions.

Subhash Sarnikar, Brihaspati V. and T. Krishna Mohan live abroad and lead quiet lives.

J.P. Ramappa and V.R.K. Prasad served as Chancellors before stepping aside.

The protégés Yasaswy mentored continue to rise.

M.R. Raghu now leads Marmore MENA Intelligence. V.P. Joy serves as Senior Vice President at Reliance Foundation. Sanjeev Varma, the editor, lives in Gurugram. A.V. Vedpuriswar has now stepped into consulting. R. Prasad is Senior Director at ICFAI.

Yasaswy's children chose their own journeys. Tejaswy leads a group of ventures out of London, while Vennela continues to work with The Art of Living Foundation. Both are still guided by the values their father lived by.

Steve Jobs once famously said: 'The people who are crazy enough to think they can change the world are the ones who do.' N.J. Yasaswy was one of them.

Jobs changed how we communicate, and Yasaswy altered how we learn. Jobs gave us tools, and Yasaswy gave us belief.

They died three days apart in October 2011—two visionaries and two revolutionaries. Neither waited for permission. Neither played it safe. Both left behind worlds that still run on the fuel of their imagination.

Today, ICFAI's real legacy isn't in numbers. It lives in the small-town student who dares to dream. In the teacher who finds meaning beyond a pay cheque. In every campus that still hums with quiet ambition.

This isn't just the story of a man who built. It's the story of someone who believed in the impossible, the improbable, and the not-yet-built. He is the man who saw tomorrow.

Epilogue
Yasaswy's Nine Codes

You've read the stories and seen the journey unfold. It's now time to step back and uncork the method behind the magic. It is a toolkit of nine principles Yasaswy lived by.

If you're building anything—a school, a start-up, an institution, a company, anything—this may be the chapter you return to most.

If there was a Michael Schumacher of Indian education, it was N.J. Yasaswy. He was always racing ahead, eyes on the curve, heart on the mission. But ICFAI wasn't racing against others. It was racing against its own ambition. Idea after idea, ICFAI expanded like a start-up on caffeine.

CODE 1: Pick Smart

Ideas know no nationality. If it works in Houston, it might work in Hyderabad.

The ICFAI Law School wasn't born in India. In the late nineties, Indian legal education was trailing global practices. The West had moved on to cyber law, patent law, and arbitration. Yasaswy sensed the shift. A small ICFAI team studied curricula from Harvard, Stanford, and Columbia, and adapted them for India. By the time others caught up, ICFAI Law School was already shaping the next decade of legal education by focusing on the convergence of law, business and technology.

CODE 2: Let Numbers Decide

Yasaswy loved ideas, but didn't fall in love with them. 'The heart can suggest,' he'd say, 'but the head must decide.'

Before IBS was launched, the team crunched the numbers. 'Let's admit five hundred students. Eighty per cent of them will clear the CFA. At nine schools that's four hundred CFAs a year.'

The same logic powered every launch—like how March did the groundwork before INC centres were chosen. For Yasaswy who admired Sun Tzu's *The Art of War*, numbers were the purest form of truth.

CODE 3: Build the Right Story

'Don't build what looks good on paper,' he said. 'Build what fits our story.'

ICFAI didn't start journals to make money. It started them to sharpen faculty minds, keep the research engine running, and quietly plant the ICFAI name on global shelves. The same applied to its Case Research Centre. The goal wasn't to beat Harvard. It was to keep ICFAI in circulation where it mattered.

When someone suggested launching a credit rating agency, Yasaswy paused: 'If our alumni are applying for jobs there, and we own it, that's a huge conflict.' He always believed that reputation is the story you protect when no one is watching.

CODE 4: Time the Trigger

Some ideas are brilliant. But timing is everything.

ICFAI had dreamed of its printing press for years, but it waited. In 2002, outsourcing costs hit ₹400 lakh. The math now made sense: invest ₹100 lakh, save ₹80 lakh a year, and earn a margin of twenty per cent. That same year, the press went live—printing journals, books and courseware at scale. Yasaswy was waiting for the moment when the numbers and the need aligned. After all, patience is also a form of speed.

CODE 5: Build Brick by Brick

In 1999, ICFAI opened a small marketing centre with eight desks. One year later, it had twenty branches.

'Don't launch like a missile,' Yasaswy would say. 'Launch like Lego. Brick by brick.'

That's how the publications evolved, too. It started with a newsletter. Then *The Analyst*. Then *The Journal of Applied Finance* and *The ICFAI Reader*. When *The Effective Executive* didn't work, he quietly pulled the plug.

'If it doesn't work, kill it. But if it does—scale it like there's no tomorrow.' Because scale without sequence is just noise.

CODE 6: Plant Oaks, Not Sprouts

With just a prospectus and a dream, he launched ICFAI Tech. This was 2002 when engineering colleges were everywhere.

'The brand, ICFAI, will work on management, maybe,' friends warned. 'But it won't work on engineering.' Yasaswy still went ahead. He believed India needed engineers beyond just the IITs and NITs.

So, he converted a disused factory into a college, hired faculty months before classes began, and got hostels ready before students arrived. It wasn't a leap of faith. It was a long, calculated bet. Because real builders think in decades, not quarters.

CODE 7: Run while Laying the Track

IBS was business at the speed of thought. Eight cities. Zero infrastructure. Yasaswy hired a motley crew—ex-bankers, professors, dreamers. Each was sent out to build a business school from scratch.

One student complained about the dust. Yasaswy told the coordinator to say: 'IIM Ahmedabad's first batch studied under trees. We're giving you walls.' Progress is never tidy.

CODE 8: Pass the Baton

Project leaders build. Operators scale. 'The guy who builds the plane shouldn't fly it,' Yasaswy said. When ICFAI Tech was launched, the founding team stepped back, and a new team was brought in to run it.

Project management is war. Profit management is peace. And they demand different temperaments. He often reminded people that Winston Churchill won the war, but lost the election in peace time.

'Horses for courses' was the mantra. Because knowing when to step aside is also leadership.

CODE 9: Experiment in Silence

Some experiments didn't need attention. They needed cover.

When ICFAI explored equity research, it didn't use its name. It called the venture Cygnus. If it clicked, they'd absorb it. If it failed, no one would remember. One project—the Securities Research Centre—did fail. It broke Yasaswy's heart. But not his spirit.

In 2003, he asked O.R.S. Rao to try again, focusing on corporates 'But let's do it quietly,' he said. 'Let the results speak.' He didn't believe in perfect plans. He believed in acting, adapting, and learning on the fly. Because the truest experiments happen before the applause.

A Playbook for the First Time

And yet, he never wrote down any of these rules. He never framed them on a wall. He never even delivered a talk along its lines. He simply lived them. What remains now are not instructions but footprints on the long road to success.

When people asked how ICFAI managed to launch so much, so fast, his answer never changed 'We don't wait for the storm to pass. We build in the rain.'

In an age of chaos, he built clarity. In a world that waits, he acted. And if you ever forget what it means to build—not for applause, but for impact—come back to these pages, and reread the nine codes. They are imprints.

Lao Tzu believed the best leaders are barely noticed—until their work is done and others say, 'We did it ourselves.' Yasaswy fits that mould. He didn't just build institutions. He built builders. And what he left behind was a philosophy written in quiet code.

It's time for the world to know the code.

Acknowledgements

In writing *The Man Who Saw Tomorrow: The Untold Story of N. J. Yasaswy*, we owe our gratitude to many.

To N.J. Yasaswy, who, though he left us in 2011, continues to inspire our work and imagination.

To Smt. Sobharani Yasaswy, for her warmth, encouragement, and gracious access to memories and materials.

To V.R. Sankara, for opening the doors of ICFAI and guiding us to authentic sources.

To N.J. Yasaswy's former colleagues, friends, and family members who shared their time and reflections.

To Yamini Chowdhury and Padma Pegu of Rupa Publications, for believing in the importance of this biography.

To Rohan Datta, for his thoughtful structural edits.

To Malaiselvan Nagarajan, for the intuition behind the cover design.

And finally, to you, the reader—thank you for choosing to spend time with this story.

Glossary

Vernacular word	Language	Meaning
Avial, Idli	Telugu	Food name
Avunu	Telugu	Yes
Babu	Telugu	Endearment for boy
Garu	Telugu	Honorific suffix
Kaisa Hai / Badiya Hai	Hindi	Hindi greeting
Main Hoon Na	Hindi	I am there for you
Mangamma Gaari Vantalu	Telugu	Mangamma's meals
Nanna Garu	Telugu	Father
Paanch	Hindi	Five
Pallu	Hindi	Sari drape end
Sari	Hindi	Indian garment

Index